Western Music

an introduction

To my dear comrade-in-art, Dr. Alan Bush

Ronald Stevenson

Western Music

an introduction

KAHN & AVERILL, LONDON

First published in 1971 by Stanmore Press Ltd
under their associated imprint: Kahn & Averill
Copyright © 1971 Ronald Stevenson
This book may not be reproduced, in whole or
in part, without permission. Application with
regard to any use of any part of this volume
should be addressed to the publishers.

The music examples listed below are reproduced by courtesy of the following publishers:

Emmanuel's *Hindu Sonatina*: Durand et Cie., Paris

Godowsky's *Gamelan* (from the *Java Suite*): Carl Fischer Inc., New York.

Grainger's *Arrival Platform Humlet*: Schott & Co., London

Hába's String Quartet, op. 87: Artia, Prague

Ho Lu-ting's *Shepherd's Pipe*: Chinese Literature Press, Peking

Schoenberg's *Walzer*, op. 23: Alfred Kalmus/Universal Edition, London & Vienna

Shostakovich's Fugue, op. 87, no. 2: Boosey & Hawkes/Leeds Music Corporation, London & New York

Strauss's *Thus Spake Zarathustra*: Leuckart, Munich

Tagore's *Though my Time has come*: Adam House, Edinburgh

Printed in England by Willmer Brothers Limited, Birkenhead

Contents

1	Music's Origins and Elements	7
2	Harmony and Polyphony in Historical Perspective	16
3	The Music of the Ancients	23
4	Plainsong	35
5	The Troubadours	41
6	Gothic Music	48
7	Flemish Music	62
8	Palestrina and his Contemporaries	67
9	The Tudor School and their Continental contemporaries	75
10	The beginnings of Opera and Ballet	83
11	The Baroque and Rococo styles	92
12	The Viennese Classics *compare*	119
13	Revolution, Romanticism, Nationalism and Realism	137
14	The Twentieth Century	166
15	Towards World Music	197
	A Brief Bibliography	209
	Acknowledgments	210
	Index	211

1 Music's Origins and Elements

'Music was born free; and to win freedom is its destiny.'
— *Busoni*

Music, like all the other arts, is a reflection of reality. It reflects not as a mirror but as a river — not a lifeless image but a quick changing one. It reflects its composer's character and environment and his relationship to society. It doesn't only reflect reality: it *transforms* it.

History is the struggle of man to comprehend, control and change nature, including human nature. Ethnography shows that the origins of music lay in magic and labour. Music plays more directly on the emotions than any other art and man's deepest and most primitive emotion is fear. Fear is indissoluble from primitive magic. In the 'space age', man lives and works in the knowledge that the process of his discovery of the universe will go on as long as the universe itself goes on, and this knowledge reduces fear. So the ancient magical origins of music are transformed through the other factor which was there in music's beginnings: labour, the primary condition of human existence.

Originally, magic and labour were united in ritualistic music accompanying the hunting of food and agricultural activity. Early peoples invested nature with magical attributes because the processes of nature were not understood, and what was unknown was occult. As nature's capacity for yielding was gradually realized, so the labour that made it yield was linked with its magic.

Music history shows these two elements of magic and labour locked in dialectical intercourse, in unity and struggle. The essence of man's thinking is contained in the law of the unity and conflict of opposites. Opposites imply contradiction and contradiction implies relative unity and absolute conflict. It is conflict which makes history move by impelling change. It is this law that transforms the old into the new, and it is as a consequence of this law that Busoni's prophecy will be fulfilled in reality.

But what is music's immediate effect on the individual listener? In his poem, *A Song for Occupations*, Walt Whitman writes: 'All music is what awakes from you when you are reminded by the instruments.' In other words it is not the instruments that matter most, not the performers, not even the composer, but all these factors taken together, projected onto the retina of music, the human brain. This is the very beginning of the listening experience, the root of music's meaning to human beings, so let us examine what *does* happen.

At the beginning of the 20th century, the Russian natural scientists Pavlov and Bekhterev explained the process. We perceive sound through the essential organ of hearing called the organ of Corti, a complex, minuscule, tunnel-like mechanism in the inner ear. In it, sound waves cause the nervous process of hearing. Through nerve fibres, auditory stimuli reach the cortex. There, analysis and synthesis of all outer stimuli take place.

The human organism itself plays a kind of music, like some unique electronic instrument. Each heart beat and muscular contraction and expansion generates biocurrents – living electricity – in the cells of the body. Scientists can each hear them on special recordings, which enable them to evaluate the condition of individual organs and of the whole organism. The properties and influences of music relate to the changes of frequencies which determine the height or depth of sound; and the direction of the sound waves is also a factor.

This knowledge has led to music therapy. Already cases of beneficial treatment of excitable children by music therapy are documented. Medical science is using ultrasonics to restore nerve tissues. Brain surgery is employing high-frequency sinusoidal sound (pure tone without overtones). It has the power to penetrate healthy tissue harmlessly, but to destroy pathological ones.

Mankind has for a long time intuitively sensed the soothing properties of nature's sounds. The influence of the sound of lapping waves or rustling trees, is not merely 'poetic' but positively therapeutic. Statistically, foresters and sailors do not suffer from occupational nervous disorders and cardiovascular diseases as much as other people do.

But what does music *mean*? There are even people who deny that it *has* meaning. But it doesn't seem intelligent to listen to whole concerts of music composed by geniuses if it is meaningless. The best answer to this question that I have ever read was written by the American orator Robert G. Ingersoll in his *Oration on Walt Whitman* in 1890:

'I believe that certain feelings and passions – joy, grief, emulation, revenge – produce certain molecular movements in the brain; that every thought is accompanied by certain physical phenomena. Now it may be that certain sounds produce the same molecular action in the brain that accompanies certain feelings, and that these sounds produce first the molecular movements, and these in their turn reproduce the feelings in motions and states of mind capable of producing the same or like molecular movements. So that what we call heroic music produces the same molecular action in the brain – the same physical changes – that are produced by the real feeling of heroism; that the sounds we call plaintive produce the same molecular movement in the brain that grief, or the twilight of grief, actually produces. There may be a rhythmical molecular movement belonging to each state of mind that accompanies each thought or passion, and it may be that music produces the same state of mind or feeling that produces the music, by producing the same molecular movements.'

A cutting from *The Times* of 29 February 1968, confirms Ingersoll's hypothesis:

'Electrical recordings taken from single cells in a cat's brain have shown the existence of cells that are active only during fighting. When the electrode is used to stimulate such cells instead of to record from them, the cat hisses or makes aggressive motions.'

Now that we have investigated music's effect upon the listener, we shall consider its constituents, the things that make it work.

Music's material is made of four elements: rhythm, melody,

harmony and polyphony. Rhythm is a succession of beats. Melody or tune is a succession of single sounds of different frequencies (frequencies being the physicist's term for the numerical method of measuring the height or depth of sound in vibration-cycles per second). Harmony is a succession of simultaneous sounds of different frequencies. Polyphony is the simultaneous sounding of melodies in different rhythms. Polyphony literally means many-voiced music. Another word for it is counterpoint. Rhythm may exist on its own, as it does in the beats of dancing feet; but melody, harmony and counterpoint cannot exist without rhythm. Wherever there is counterpoint there is harmony, but harmony can exist without counterpoint.

Rhythm is music's heart-beat. It is made by the foot on the earth, the hammer on the anvil, the waves on the shore, sound on silence. Like the heart, rhythm can palpitate with emotion. It can be onomatopoeic, imitating the ticking of a clock, horses' hooves, thunder, or the crash of tidal wave on rock. But it can be more subtly and profoundly suggestive of the rocking motion of the sea from which all life came, or of the rocking motion of a mother's arms as she sings a lullaby to her baby. Rhythm can reproduce any emotion suggested by whatever is rhythmic in nature.

There is mechanical rhythm and vital rhythm. Mechanical rhythm has motion but vital rhythm has also emotion. Mechanical rhythm moves in one sense; vital rhythm moves in both senses.

The instruments of rhythm are many and among the most ancient and primitive. They range from those which produce the most delicate sounds to those which make the most deafening din: from South African ankle-rattles made from the sewn, dried skin of springbok ears filled with small pieces of ostrich shell or pebbles – to the large sheets of tin shaken before the microphones of radio stations, to imitate thunder in broadcast plays. Between those extremes there are the clapping hands and stamping of feet; hand-clappers made from leather strips nailed to flat slabs of wood or made from rib-bones of cattle; the most primitive drum, a hollowed tree trunk covered with a membrane, struck by the hand and amassed into a primitive percussion-band according to the sizes of the trees used; the drum of hide stretched across a resonator such as a wooden water-jug or milk-jug or clay pot or the shell of the giant bush-tortoise, and struck by the hands or by sticks; xylophones with calabash or gourd resonators underneath the primitive keyboard of wood slabs beaten with sticks covered with balls of sinew or rubber; the tribal 'hand piano' made from a rectangular piece of hollowed wood with affixed metal tongues plucked by the thumbnails; gongs and bells – the music of ritual and fires and war and peace; clashing swords, the earliest cymbals – the music of battle. The evolution of rhythmic instruments is from jungle to factory, from primitive communications to television, and its extent may be judged by a comparison of the exhibits in an ethnomusicological museum and the array of a symphony orchestra's or jazz band's percussion section.

Rhythm is based on national characteristics of deportment and dancing. It is this fact which makes a Polish mazurka different from a French minuet or a Viennese waltz, though a repeated pattern of three beats is common to them all.

If rhythm is music's life-beat, heart-pulse, hand-clap or foot-stamp, melody is music's individual voice. Melody is most movingly expressed by the human voice because this is the organ which must inevitably convey the subtlest shades of human psychology. Though all instruments, with the exception of some percussion instruments, can play melody, it is the wind instruments (woodwind and brass) which are the most essentially melodic, because they are only capable of emitting single notes; and melody is by definition a succession of single notes. The human voice itself is a wind instrument, and the earliest wind instruments were modelled on it: the bagpipe, for instance, which substitutes a chanter for the windpipe, a reed for the larynx, and a bag or bladder for the lungs. As the bagpipe was modelled on the voice, so the modern pneumatic organ, with its giant pipes and bellows, is an extension of the bagpipe. The evolution of wind instruments is from the classical pastoral scene to the workshops of such perfectionists as the Belgian Sax and the German Wieprecht in the nineteenth century. In the present age, wind-music has been cultivated by the U.S.A. more than any other country. The American wind-band (consisting of full consorts – complete family groups – of brass and woodwind instruments) is a national institution and is found in every high-school, college and university. Its body of sound is far more flexible and expressive because its volume-range is far greater than that of the symphony orchestra.

Melody is based on national characteristics of speech inflexion which, when sung, determine melodic intonation. Other determining factors are derived from national characteristics of deportment and dancing, which affect melodic contour as the force of gravity affects the flight of a bird. Rhythm keeps music earth-bound; melody aspires. Rhythm is an animal function; melody is humanistic and spiritual.

If melody is music's individual voice, harmony is its corporate voice and polyphony its interplay of many voices. Harmony and polyphony are produced by choirs or groups of instruments or by keyboard or string instruments which, due to their complexity of construction, are capable of producing two or more notes simultaneously, which a human voice or a woodwind or brass instrument cannot do.

The evolution of keyboard instruments spans from the Babylonian dulcimer to the modern grand piano perfected in the workshops of Steinway and Bechstein in nineteenth century Germany, and the development of string instruments is from the primitive hunter's bow to the Cremonan workshop of Stradivarius in early eighteenth century Italy.

National characteristics in harmony and polyphony are determined by national characteristics of rhythm and melody. So music varies from nation to nation. It also varies from continent to continent. Western music, the subject of this book, may only be understood in perspective with the musics of other cultures: we can only get it in focus against that background. On different continents, different elements of music have been developed.

In Africa, rhythm has been developed far more than the other musical elements. Climate, geographical factors and tribal customs have determined this development. Over much of Africa, climatic conditions encourage nudism, and nudism encourages freedom of movement expressed in dancing. The primitive economy of the African jungles and plains has provided the materials for the making of percussion instruments of wood and hide; and tribal customs and communications employ percussion instruments to accompany ritualistic dancing and as a kind of primeval 'morse code'. Because Africa has not yet emerged from tribalism, there is a fallacious notion among some Europeans that African music is rudimentary. But African rhythm is the most complex in the world. In comparison with it, European rhythm is rudimentary.

Melody has been developed most in India. Indian melody has a much richer 'vocabulary' of notes than any other melody, and a freer, improvisatory nature. Traditional Asian music in general is essentially melodic and rhythmic and not harmonic or polyphonic. India has 287 different kinds of drum, but the rhythm of Indian music is subservient to its melody. In this it is the opposite of African music, in which melody is subservient to rhythm. The Hindu raga-singer, a highly skilled professional, can sing *twenty-two* notes to an octave (from 'low do' to 'high do'), whereas the Western amateur finds it difficult to sing *do-ray-me-fa-so-la-te-do* – a mere 8 notes – in tune; and the professional singer finds it difficult to sing 12 divisions of the octave. (Raga, by the way, is the name given to the Indian scale-system. The raga-singer can sing 22 notes to the octave, but he doesn't generally do this. What he does is to select various scales from the 22 notes as the basic material – the raga – for his improvisation.) It is the climate, geography, basic economy, religion and language which have determined the remarkable melodic development of Indian music. The snows of the Himalayan foothills enforce solitude, and solitude induces meditation; Indian religions channel meditation and develop subtle mental control over the body, one aspect of which is the ability of the raga-singer to produce such a finely differentiated melody. Another factor is the complex influence of India's languages on its music. It is not surprising to find such complex melody when one realizes that there are no fewer than 147 distinct languages recorded as vernacular in India!

What differentiates European music (and its extension, American music) from the music of Africa or Asia is Europe's development of harmony and polyphony. This has been moulded by the forms of Christian worship and by large-scale industry. The Christian religion has organized choral harmony and polyphony more than any other religion has, and industry has helped to build and finance the institution of the modern symphony orchestra, which, apart from the massed choir, is music's principle medium for the realization of harmony and polyphony on a grand scale. The close-knit structure of European society, resulting from industry's effect on population, has also encouraged the cultivation of music composed for small groups of instrumentalists (chamber music or room music, as distinct from concert-hall music).

Western music has rhythm, of course, but it is simple in comparison with African rhythm; and it has melody, but this is simple in comparison with Indian melody. The history of Western music is largely the history of harmony and polyphony. Indeed, from the Renaissance onwards, Western music has progressed in alternating phases of polyphony and harmony. In these alternating phases we see again the law of the unity and conflict of opposites operating, impelling change and transforming the old into the new. Polyphony and harmony are united in so far as they are both concepts in terms of multiple sounds; but they are opposites in that harmony is monolithic blocks of sound, whereas polyphony is the interplay of strands of sound.

Renaissance polyphony reached its apex in 16th century Rome, in the music of Palestrina.

The school of *nuova musica* ('new music') founded by Peri and Caccini in Florence in 1600, reacted against the polyphonic austerity of Palestrina and, employing a harmonic idiom, founded opera.

Reformation polyphony reached its apex in mid-18th century Leipzig, in the music of Bach.

The successive generations developed an harmonic technique which enabled Haydn to found the symphony in late 18th century Vienna.

As the school of Viennese classicism developed, it became more polyphonic and culminated in Mozart's *Jupiter* Symphony (1788) and the Fugue from Beethoven's *Hammerklavier* Sonata (1819).

The early Romantics (Berlioz, Meyerbeer, Chopin, Liszt and others), centred in Paris, re-emphasized harmony.

Polyphony was re-asserted by the late Romantics, particularly Brahms and Wagner; the centre of activity now moving from France to Germany.

And so we come to the present age, when, as we shall discover in the later chapters, the situation has become more complex.

The transformation of the old into the new may be seen not only in epochs of music history but in the corpus of an individual composer; and the greater the composer, the clearer it is seen. The consummation of a great creative career is generally manifest in an increase of polyphonic invention and content. This is seen – or rather, heard – even in the works of a composer whose usual mode of expression is polyphonic: compare early and late Bach, for instance.

Recapitulating the opening idea of this chapter; if music is a reflection of reality, it follows that the greatest composer is he whose music is the truest reflection of reality. Reality, to the realist, is 'things as they are'. To the prophet who ventures into the future from a knowledge of past and present, reality is also 'things as they shall be'. The reflection of reality for most people – even most creative artists – is conditioned and limited by the spirit of the age. It is only a genius of the first magnitude who can project his art into another age. He does this by virtue of the humanity in his art, not by its superficial technique; because humanity is the one factor common to all ages.

Referring to the nature of music as we have studied it in its different elements, we may also say that the most complete composer is he whose work presents rhythm, melody, harmony and polyphony in equipose, developed to the limits of his particular culture.

Remembering what has been said in this chapter about the artist's relationship to society and the national roots of art, we may further say that the greatest composer is he who gives back to society a thousandfold what he has absorbed from it and whose national roots are deepest and whose universal aspiration is highest. The great composer moves the listener to a revaluation of life and moves a younger composer to even greater achievement.

2 Harmony and Polyphony in Historical Perspective

The history of Western music consists broadly of alternating periods in which either harmony or polyphony dominates. It is not a question of neatly codifying music. The ebb and flow of music history implies spiritual and social upheavals, crosscurrents, antagonisms and conflicts rather than complacent parallel columns of comparative data in a scholarly appendix. Before exploring the periods in separate chapters, it would seem desirable to get music history into focus. This can best be done by comparative examples. If one can learn what makes 16th century polyphony different from 18th or 20th century polyphony, and what makes 17th century harmony different from 19th century harmony, the more detailed study of the separate periods, undertaken in later chapters, will stand out in sharper definition.

In his *History of Musical Language*, Maurice Emmanuel gives the following example of how harmony has been extended throughout history, by the addition of more notes, piled up in thirds:

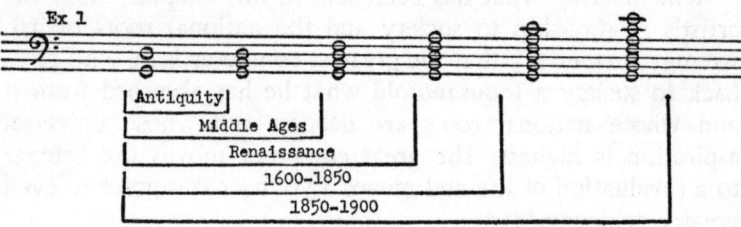

To this I would add

HARMONY AND POLYPHONY IN HISTORICAL PERSPECTIVE 17

Ex 2

for about 1900, or shortly after, Scriabin, Busoni and Schoenberg began to construct harmony on the piling-up of fourths rather than thirds.

The last two examples – Emmanuel's and mine – should be used as terms of reference.

The drone fifth – antiquity's only harmony – persists in Celtic bagpipe-music and in Indian raga-music.

The distinguishing factor between the polyphony or the harmony of different periods is the treatment of dissonance. Don't think of a dissonance or discord as an *ugly* sound, but as a sound that needs another sound to make it complete. A consonance or concord is a complete sound which needs no other to make it complete. This concept serves up to the 20th century. In the present century the polarity of discord versus concord has been reduced.

We'll start with polyphony. Our first example is from Palestrina (16th century):

Ex 3

There are two cases of dissonance here (I and II). In each case the dissonance (D) is prepared (P) by a consonance and resolved (R) by a consonance. A resolution is the *completion* of a dissonance. The two simultaneous notes of dissonance at ID are not actually struck together; neither are the two simultaneous notes at IID. The blow is softened by one of the notes being carried over ('tied') from the preparation, in each case. 'Percussed' (i.e. struck) dissonance is foreign to 16th century polyphony. Try to imagine these prepared and resolved dissonances as miniature 'suspension bridges' in the music. The picture in your mind will then be:

The music flows along and every so often there is a little 'suspension bridge'; under it the music continues to flow like water.

Now compare that with the next example, from Bach (18th century):

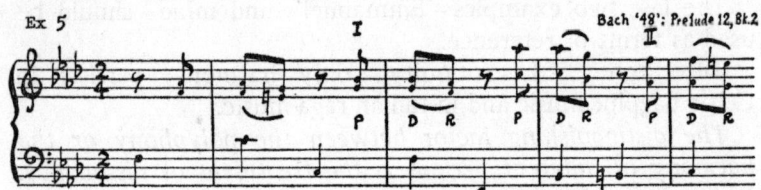

Here the dissonance is percussed. Also, at I and II, Bach prepares his dissonance by another dissonance, whereas Palestrina prepared his dissonance by a consonance; but both Palestrina and Bach resolve their dissonance on to a consonance. Bach sometimes employed *un*percussed dissonance, like Palestrina, but it is Bach's use of *percussed* dissonance that makes his music different from Palestrina's.

Our next example is from Shostakovich (20th century):

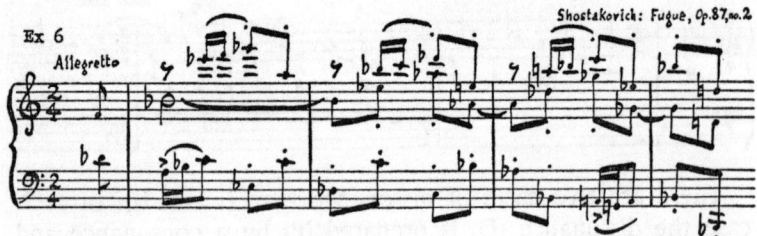

Here there are dissonances all the time until the last bar, and yet, by employing varying degrees of dissonant tension, Shostakovich has produced a contraction and extension feeling which propels the music with a kind of athletic 'muscularity'. Contemporary composers sometimes resolve dissonance (either percussed or unpercussed) but it is their use of *un*resolved dissonance which differentiates their music from earlier music.

I have quoted only one example each from the 16th, 18th and 20th centuries. Beethoven's treatment of dissonance lies somewhere between Bach and Wagner; Wagner's lies somewhere between Beethoven's and the emancipation of dissonance in the present century.

To achieve clarity I have concentrated on the one aspect of dissonance. Of course, this cannot be isolated from other aspects of music: they all interpenetrate. A comprehensive study of music must consider the many ways in which the different musical elements react upon each other. In a book like this, such subtleties can only be suggested.

Palestrina's was music of euphony. Beauty of sound was a cult in the 16th century. The Church of Rome encouraged composers to write liturgical music which would assist the act of worship; that is, other-world music, with little or nothing to remind people of the frictions of living in *this* world. True, Palestrina used unpercussed dissonance to express the Passion of Christ: the Danish scholar Knud Jeppesen has devoted a large volume to a study of Palestrina's expressive use of dissonance. But it's generally implicit, not explicit dissonance. Euphony ran all through Palestrina's music, not just in the way he smoothed the edges of his discords. There was euphony in the flow of the rhythm, in the succession of voices taking up the theme, in the intermingling of voices. There was euphony in the melody, which moved within a compass dictated by what was easily singable. It was melody which never risked any wide leaps which were difficult to sing. And there was euphony in the harmony, which used a limited number of chords, so that there was never any outburst of colour. Sixteenth century music is like architecture built in stone: sometimes in monolithic blocks, more often intricately carved, but always austere.

As music developed, the art emancipated itself from the dictates of the Church. Mankind gradually asserted itself: no easy thing. It is precisely the quest for expressive human emotions and concepts in sound which is the reason why dissonance has played an ever greater role in music. The emancipation of dissonance stands in the history of music as a symbol of the prime fact of the human condition – struggle.

Music for religious worship has negated or minimized

human concepts in sound and has subjugated them to the contemplation of more abstract concepts. Some liturgical music is among the most beautiful in the world. The human mind is so constituted that it can express itself even within dogmatic confines; which is, when you think of it, a testimony to the power of human thought.

Now we consider harmony, with examples from periods in which harmony has predominated over polyphony. (This statement must be qualified in the case of the 20th century, in which harmony cannot be said to predominate over polyphony.) Refer each example back to the 'ground plan' at the beginning of this chapter.

If the above examples are assimilated and supplemented by hearing more music, similarly compared, the reader should be able, on hearing music of different periods, to distinguish between them.

Emmanuel's 'ground plan' of history's harmony, given at the beginning of this chapter, shows a process of gradual *selective* accumulation which can be shown in every aspect of music.

Aboriginal rhythm is repetitive and its melody consists of very few notes in reiterated phrases. The music of some 20th century composers, by contrast, contains non-repetitive rhythms and phrases which consist of all twelve semitones.

Sixteenth century rhythm is made from seven basic metric units. It subdivides the whole note of four steady beats (say two beats per second) into halves, quarters and eighths. This gives us:

Ex 10

In addition, there are notes prolonged by half their value:

Ex 11

The melodic vocabulary of 16th century music comprises seven notes. This fundamental simplicity is dictated by the needs of the human voice, for 16th century music was predominantly vocal.

By the 18th century, the development of instrumental music multiplied the use of very rapid notes, for instruments other than the voice can perform more rapid sequences of notes than the voice can. And with this increase of the vocabulary of metre came more complex rhythms: the employment of subdivisions of a beat into *three* units within a general framework of beats subdivided into *two* units.

With the 19th century (particularly in Brahms) subdivisions of beats into two's and three's, which had been previously juxtaposed, were now more frequently superimposed. From the 18th century onwards, the melodic vocabulary consists of twelve notes, whereas before it had only seven as a norm, with the extra five (which complete the twelve) used relatively infrequently.

In terms of social structure, music's increasing complexity mirrors the change from agrarian society, through industrial society, to the present technological society, and this is the main distinction between contemporary Western and Eastern civilization, though the gap is narrowing.

3 The Music of the Ancients

The Ancients: a subject shrouded in obscurity which academic circumlocution generally reduces to total eclipse! And the trouble is, the further back you go in history, the further East you go and denser grows the fog of the language barrier. The Celts, who now inhabit the North-West corner of Europe, originated in the Caucasus 3,000 years ago. And so we glimpse history's perspective, down through Byzantines, Romans, Greeks, Egyptians, Hebrews, Indians and Chinese. Concerning the music of the Sumerian Ur-race nobody can say anything.

I'll start with the Celts because some of their music is the only ancient musical style which is still extant in the Western world. Celtic music is largely ignored. It is this penumbra of ignorance which has helped to preserve it, if not in its pristine state, at least in a state which is demonstrably ancient. Another reason for dealing with it first is that it unites features which are found separately in other ancient musics.

The Celtic music to which I refer is the *Ceòl Mór*, which is Scottish Gaelic for 'the Great Music', a designation which distinguishes it from the 'small music' of the Celts. Broadly, it is the same distinction as that between 'serious' and 'light' music. The *Ceol Mor* is the classical music of Scotland, just as raga-music is the classical music of India. This Great Music is played on solo bagpipes. It is emphatically not folk music. There is nothing primitive about it. It is highly sophisticated. Comparatively few pipers can play the Great Music, because of its technical difficulty. Another name for it is *piobaireachd*, which is phoneticised as 'pibroch' (the 'i' pronounced as 'ee' and accentuated; the 'ch' pronounced as in the

Scottish 'loch'). Rather than repeating the unfamiliar words *Ceòl Mór*, we shall employ the slightly better-known word, pibroch.

Pibroch is played on the great Highland bagpipes ('great' distinguishes it from the smaller Lowland pipes). The Highland pipes comprise a chanter, that is a pipe with holes played by finger manipulation; a bag to supply a constant stream of air (like the bellows of an organ); a mouth piece through which the piper transmits the air; and three drones – two tenor drones and a bass drone. To-day the tenor drones are supposed to be tuned in unison to 'A'  and the bass drone tuned an octave lower. I say 'supposed' to be because in practice they are generally tuned to something nearer B flat (possibly through the modern practice of pipe-bands playing with military bands, most of the instruments of which are in the key of B flat). The ancient pipers traditionally tuned their drones dissonantly, so that their sound would carry further over the mountains than they would if tuned consonantly. The bass drone was introduced much later than the two tenor drones, probably about 1745, when the pipes began to augment the military band.

The pipe scale is:

Ex 12

This scale comprises a pentatonic mode (notes 1, 2, 3, 5, 6; 1 and 2 being repeated an octave higher as 8 and 9) plus two microtones (notes 4 and 7) which are approximately a quarter-tone sharp (indicated by the cross). This scale is the only instance of microtonal music indigenous to Britain. By microtonal music, I mean music the melodic intervals of which are less than a semitone, that is, less than the distance between two adjacent keys on a piano. Microtonal music is therefore impossible to play on a piano. The structure of this scale is related to the structure of the Scottish Gaelic language. Scots Gaelic, as an Indo-European language, contains a main vocabulary of European-rooted words with a residual element of Sanskrit words. Visitors to Scotland generally hear the word *ceilidh* sooner or later. This is one of the Sanskrit words: the same word exists in Sanskrit as *khéli*, meaning a musical evening. The pentatonic scale contained within the pipe scale is comparable to the European words in the Gaelic language and the two microtones are the residual 'Sanskrit' element.

Pibroch is unlike other Western instrumental music and like all Eastern music in four respects: it is purely melodic and rhythmic, that is, it has neither harmony nor counterpoint and, apart from the drones, is unaccompanied; it was transmitted by oral tradition and not written down till the 19th century; its nature is improvisational; its form that of accumulatively ornamental variations.

Most standard histories of music give the English composer Hugh Aston, who died circa 1503, as 'the inventor of instrumental composition' and 'the inventor of variation form' (Grove Dictionary). These statements are erroneous. In Africa I have heard ages-old variation-form (to be precise, passacaglia-form) in the marimba-bands of illiterate Bantu tribesmen. Variation-form is as germane to man's music-making as it is to variants in animal-breeding, in horticulture, or, indeed, in the racial interpenetration of mankind itself. It is basic to music as it is to life. In the Lady Chapel of Rosslyn, Midlothian (Scotland) there is a sculpted angel-bagpiper, which antiquarians date as circa 1440. In chronological connection with this there is a pibroch entitled *Pibroch of Donnel Dubh* ('Black Donnel') which commemorates the Battle of Inverlochy (1431). Though this composition post-dates the Battle, its existence argues a tradition which dates back at least to that historical event. The 14th century French chronicler, Froissart mentions the 'Great War pipe' at the Battle of Otterburn (1388). In Edinburgh, in the National Museum of Antiquities of Scotland, there is preserved a set of bagpipes which bears the date 1409, an oft-quoted and partially restored relic. The antiquarian, Angus Mackay, records that Iain Odhar ('John of the dun hue'), the 16th century sire of the MacCrimmon family, (hereditary pipers to the MacLeod of Skye,) was the teacher of Donald Mòr (c. 1570–1640) some of whose pibrochs have been preserved orally and finally notated. This Donald Mòr ('Big Donald') was the father of Patrick Mòr, the composer of one of the greatest pibrochs, *Cumha na Cloinne*

('Lament for the Children'). From these antecedents it is obvious that the earliest perfected solo instrumental variation-form in Europe was the Scottish pibroch. The almost exclusive cultivation of keyboard music by the upper classes in leading European countries over the past four centuries has blinded music historians to this fact.

The music of ancient Rome and of Greece was heptatonic (based on a seven-note scale). So is the pipe-scale heptatonic, that is, it has seven different notes, though two are repeated in the higher octave, making nine notes in all. The music of Egypt and India was microtonic (based on scales with intervals less than the Western semitone). The pipe-scale is also partially microtonic. The music of ancient China was pentatonic (consisting of five notes). The pipe-scale also contains a pentatonic structure, if we exclude the two microtones. Therefore, the scale of the great Highland bagpipe is in itself a microcosmic amalgam of the scalic structures of music's history, both occidental and oriental.

Both Byzantine and Roman music were ramifications of Greek music. Byzantine music was that of the primitive Eastern Church. It has persisted down to our own time, just as Gregorian chant has in the Roman Church, and coalesces Greek, Hebrew, Syrian and Armenian strains. It is rhythmically very free, even a-rhythmic, that is, accent plays no significant part in it. In this and in its ornamental melodic line, it has much in common with pibroch. Another feature common to both Byzantine chants and pibroch is the drone. The Byzantine chant is sung by a solo cantor, whose melodic line can thus be rhythmically unhindered by the exigencies of choral ensemble. This solo melody is underpinned by a choral drone. The occasional employment of an augmented second 𝄞 in Byzantine chant points to semitic influence.

Another melodic influence was the Greek modes (scales of different melodic inflexions). The subject of Byzantine music is extremely specialized. Readers wishing to explore it further should consult the writings of Dr. Egon Wellesz, the Schoenberg pupil, who has for many years been resident in Oxford.

Roman culture was a spoiling (in both senses) of Greek culture. As music under both cultures was chiefly an adjunct to theatre, the difference between Greece and Rome, in modern terms, resembled that between the European tradition of theatre (from Shakespeare to Shaw) and the American tradition of the Hollywood or Broadway 'spectacular'. The Roman *satura* was an entertainment in the spirit of the modern revue 'a medley of invective, imitation and music' (Wells: *The Outline of History*). The *vates*, a bardic figure, sang sarcastic songs to the plebeians, interlarded with orations, laments and a smattering of religious liturgy (when the Roman Empire was crumbling and Christianity was in the ascendant.)

The importance of the Greeks in the history of music is that they were the first to systematize the art and, especially, to relate it to physics. They founded the science of acoustics, which in the 19th century was to be developed by the German scientist, Helmholtz (1821–94). The initiator of this scientific investigation of music was Pythagoras, who was born in Samos, Greece in the 6th century B.C. He lived under the tyrantship of Polycrates, ally of Amasis, King of Egypt. Through this Graeco-Egyptian *entente*, Pythagoras is supposed to have travelled to Egypt and to have adapted Egyptian mathematics (which applied to pyramidal architecture and agriculture) to music. Ultimately, he left Samos because he found its rule oppressive, and he settled for 20 years in Croton, a Greek city in Southern Italy. He returned to Greece to die. 'Pythagoras discovered the simple numerical relations of musical intervals' (Bertrand Russell: *Wisdom of the West*). They were shown in the ratios 2:4 and 3:1 which meant that a full string sounds the fundamental note; clamped at ¾ it sounds the note four notes higher than the fundamental; when this shortened string is clamped at ⅔ of its length it sounds the note five notes higher still; this final length, being ½ of the original, it sounds an octave (8 notes) above it.

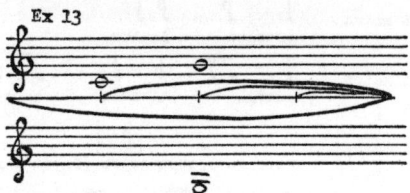

Pythagoras represented numbers by arrangements of pebbles;

the Latin word 'calculation' meaning 'a handling of pebbles'. Apollo, symbol of ordered beauty, was the Pythagorean god. This Apollonian influence runs all through the rationalistic theology of Greece, which distinguishes it from Eastern mysticism. In a sense, although world events of the 20th century often caricature democracy, we are still living in the Democritan period of history; for one line of development is discernable from Democritus of Abdera (North Greece) who lived in the 5th century B.C. and who developed the atomic theory, the implications of which have been realized in the 20th century. The same might be said of the relationship between the acoustics of Pythagoras and electronic music.

Aristoxenus of Tarentum (4th century B.C.), a peripatetic philosopher, pupil of Aristotle, was the first to codify the elements of Greek music. Modern notation fractionalises a 'gross' maximum unit, the semibreve or whole-note, which is divided into 2 minims (half-notes); 4 crotchets (quarter-notes); 8 quavers (eighth-notes), etc. But the Greeks, on the contrary, began with the *minimum* duration, the rhythmically indivisible 'atom', and built up rhythms on this basis, which gave them more rhythmic liberty than is possible by the mathematical subdivision of a note of maximum length.

Their basic metres were named after human activity: the *trochee*, two running feet; the *dactyl*, the phalanxes of the finger, moving from the joints; the *spondee*, two long quaffs (the rhythm of a solemn toast); the *anapaest*, blows in fisticuffs; the *iambus*, an assault. The principle metre in Greek music was named 'Cretan' after the island and another metre was named 'Ionic' after the Ionians who are thought to have originated in Attica.

The main Hellenic rhythms are:

THE MUSIC OF THE ANCIENTS   29

The above examples are given in modern notation. The Greeks used alphabetical notation.

Just as the Greek conception of rhythmic structure is the reverse of ours – they build up their rhythm from its shortest unit, we break down ours from its longest duration – so the Greek conception of the scale differs from ours. The principle scale of Ancient Greece was the Dorian mode. They thought of it from top to bottom, whereas we think of the principle European scale from the end of the Middle Ages, the Major scale, as from the lowest note to the highest. A comparison will reveal that they are similar in construction, but each is an inversion of the other:

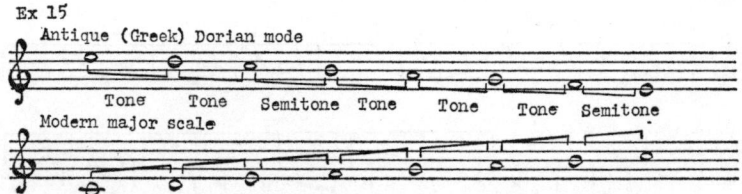

The Greek modes were named after regions or colonies of Greece and each had a different character deriving from its place of origin, in the same way that, in architecture, the Doric capital is stout, the Ionic, graceful, and the Corinthian, florid.

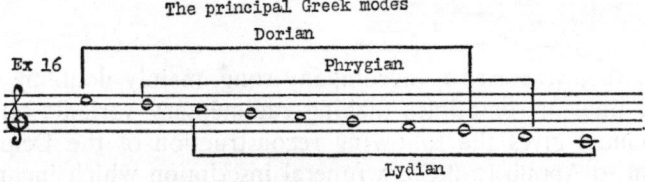

The Phrygian mode derived from Phrygia, a large Greek colony in Asia minor, whose inhabitants were called 'freemen' by the Greeks. The Lydian mode derived from Lydia, another district of Asia Minor. There were variants of the three principle modes, but we need not explain them in a book of this nature. Each mode was considered to have a mood or 'ethos' of its own: the Dorian, brave; the Phrygian, dignified; the Lydian, voluptuous. At different periods of history, the names of the modes were re-shuffled. The above classification is according to Ptolemy (the mathematician Claudius Ptolemaeus, who flourished c. 140–160 A.D.).

The two principle instruments of ancient Greece were the aulos (a single or double flute) and the cither (the flat-backed lute with wire strings, played with a quill plextrum; the forerunner of the zither).

Ancient Greece knew only melody and rhythm, no harmony or counterpoint. The aulos could indicate a rudimentary harmony, however, by droning on one pipe and playing a tune on the other. Gevaert made the following hypothetical reconstruction of a Greek melody for double aulos:

The zither was used to accompany song, mainly doubling the vocal line, or sometimes making rudimentary variants on it. Emmanuel gives the following reconstruction of the Delphic Hymn to Apollo (2 B.C.), a funeral inscription which includes the lines 'Life is brief; look to thine end.' The form is built up of strophic couplets. The Hymn opens like this:

Music played an essential role in Greek drama. The earliest form of Greek drama (pre-700 B.C.) was improvised and consisted of song, ritual and dance. The Dionysian chorus chanted in strict metre. The content was mythological. C. 600 B.C. Thespis introduced a solo actor. C. 450 B.C. Aeschylus introduced a second actor; C. 420 B.C. Sophocles introduced a third actor, (the 'human triangle'). Aeschylus innovated individual dialogue; Sophocles the dramatic plot, psychologically delineated. The word 'tragedy' originally meant a goat-song, from ancient chants accompanying the ritual sacrifice of goats to Dionysus, god of Nature. Tragedies were trilogies, three self-contained related plays 'to excite pity and terror' (Aristotle). The family was the fulcrum of Greek life, conceived in the hierarchies of gods, royalty and citizenry. Plato's *Republic* incidentally considers the influence of music on society.

The earliest reference to Hebrew music is in Exodus XV, the 'song of Moses', *Sirath Hayyam* (Song at the Sea). There is a tradition that the following ancient Sephardic melody is the one sung by Miriam:

The opening and closing phrases, moving within the ambit of three notes, is characteristic of the most ancient Hebrew cantillations (the Hebrew chants).

The oldest surviving instrument used in the Synagogue is the Sofar (ram's horn). The following sofar-calls are taken from the Jewish Encyclopedia, vol. XI:

Davidic Psalms were chanted to the psaltery (a small harp). References to instruments abound in the Bible: 1 Samuel, X, 5; 1 Chronicles, XIII, 8, XV, 16–25, XVI, 4–43, XXI, 15, XXV, 1–31; 2 Chronicles, V, 12–14, VII, 6; Psalm 127; Psalm 150, etc.

The Jewish cantillation system was practised according to strictly defined rules. Finger movements indicated the pitch of notes.

The interval of the augmented second (already mentioned in considering Byzantine music) is characteristic of one type of Hebrew melody, suggesting Arabic influence.

When we come to the music of ancient Egypt, we are on quicksand. We have a few museum specimens and wall paintings: the rest is conjecture. The oldest existing musical instrument in the world, an Egyptian lyre, is housed in the Berlin Museum. It is about 4,000 years old, dating from the period immediately prior to the expulsion of the Hyksor or 'Shepherd' kings. The Florence Museum contains a flute dating from 1700–1600 B.C. It was found in the royal tombs at Thebes and has a chromatic scale. Some commentators aver that the music of ancient Egypt was in thirds of tones and induced trance. The mystery plays in propitiation of Osiris (god of the underworld) and Isis his sister and wife (goddess of fertility) were, from the evidence of wall-paintings, accompanied by orchestras of harps and flutes, the chanting of men's voices and the rattle of the sistrum.

Coptic music coalesced indigenous Egyptian elements with early Christian chants.

Babylonian bas-relief sculptures frequently show the dulcimer, an instrument with a hollow body covered with parchment, strung with many strings and struck by a stick. This is the prototype of the pianoforte.

Chapter I referred to both Indian and Chinese music. A lengthy exegesis of oriental music hardly comes within the province of a book on Western music; though an adumbration of Asian music can afford perspective and more clearly define the nature of Western music by comparison.

The 13th century scholar Sarngadeva enumerated 264 ragas, though only 72 are extant. Dr. Ananda Coomaraswamy graphically describes a raga as a 'melody-mould'. It is at once the basic shape and the vocabulary from which the Indian musician improvises. Each time of day has its appropriate raga. Through the concerts of the sitarist, Ravi Shankar, and other Indian musicians, Western audiences are beginning to familiarise themselves with classical Indian music as it survives after many centuries. The sitar is a kind of Indian guitar. It is accompanied by the tabla, a drum which is made in large and small sizes. The smaller tabla is tuned to the keynote and the pitch of the larger tabla is varied by pressure from the heel of the hand. Another instrument used to accompany the sitar and/or singing is the tambura, a droning string instrument, which plays a similar role to the drones of a Scottish bagpipe.

Classical music of China is made out of five 'gapped' scales, each of five notes. (A 'gapped' scale has a leap in it as well as steps.) These five scales with their Chinese names are:

Ex 21

Chinese pentatonic melody is repetitive and consists of phrases which pivot round a centre-note, whereas the pentatonic melody of Scotland or Hungary or of the American negroes is wider-ranging and less repetitive (though each has its own characteristics). Ancient Chinese music was classified according to the material used in instrument-making: the sound of skin, of stone, of metal, of clay, of silk, of wood, of bamboo, of gourd. The *kin* is an instrument with a large framework, on which are hung stones of different sizes, struck with a hammer. Bells provide another characteristic sonority of Chinese music. The balance of sections in a Chinese orchestra is diametrically opposed to that of a Western orchestra. They have a preponderance of percussion over winds and strings, whereas our symphony orchestra reverses the ratio.

The lineage of Peking opera (a highly stylized dramatic form) antecedes Western opera (which was founded in 1600) by many centuries.

Philosophers and revolutionaries, men of thought and men of action alike, from both East and West, throughout history, have realized music's latent moral influence and its unifying force in society. The following lines from a musico-philosophic poem by Wang Yu-Ching, written in the 12th century A.D. (Sung dynasty) have a timeless chime about them:

> O Music, great unity!
> Thou revealest thyself
> As the totality
> Of classical beauty.

POSTSCRIPT TO THE MUSIC OF THE ANCIENTS. Chapter 3 deals with the matrix cultures of antiquity. Of South East Asia, I have dealt only with China because Chinese culture was basic to neighbouring countries, including Japan. Naturally, each country developed its own music, but the South East Asian geographical complex, including many island cultures, shared with China a basically pentatonic music. Japan developed variants of the Chinese pentatonic system: you can play a Chinese five-note scale on the black keys of the piano, but a Japanese five-note scale on four black keys and one white one — what might be termed *inflected* pentatony. Some form of pentatony is basic also to the musics of Indonesia, Melanesia, Micronesia and Polynesia. The music of the Australian aborigines, one of the earliest cultures extant, is also often pentatonic; characterised by a descending melodic graph, beginning with a high wail and gradually falling through iterative phrases. The gypsies, who entered Europe from India in the 15th century, introducing themselves as Egyptian penitents bound for Rome, have no music of their own; but their genius for improvisation, both as nomads and as musical performers, stamps their freedom on the music they adopt. Having no need of brick walls, they are resented by many urban dwellers; and the gypsy's music is often too wild for domesticated tastes. But the gypsies are music's 'harmonious blacksmiths'. They have brought something of the East to the West.

4 Plainsong

Plainsong is the classical and most ancient music of the Church of Rome. It consists of unaccompanied, rhythmically free and melodically strict music sung in unison (all the singers together on each note) by men's and boys' voices, women being traditionally excluded from participation by ecclesiastic law. It is therefore an example of what is called 'monody', single line music. Plainsong is some of the most impersonal music, but, for that reason, I should like to begin this chapter with a personal reminiscence.

During 1955 I was living in Rome, engaged in research on music. Every Sunday morning, I attended St. Peter's, not out of allegiance to the faith but just to hear the plainsong. It was a strangely moving experience to enter the old Cathedral from the hubbub of the streets of modern Rome. St. Peter's is not, to my way of thinking, as inducive to meditation as, for example, York Minster. The High Altar over the traditional tomb of St. Peter is a baroque edifice with serpentine columns in ebony and gold, like writhing pythons. For somebody from the North, the whole feeling of the architecture is almost 'operatic'. Indeed, there was for me almost as great a contrast between the architecture of St. Peter's and its plainsong as there was between the noise of the streets and the quiet of the Cathedral. I used to sit there entranced by what seemed like an incense of sound rising to the great dome. I use that analogy because plainsong conveys that same 'other-worldliness' as the aroma of incense. My reason for this digression is to point out that the only way to experience such music is to go and hear it in a church. Only in that way will this impersonal music become a personal part of one's experience. Listening to plainsong on gramophone records is futile, unless you've heard it also in a church. There are two factors involved here: acoustics and atmosphere. Cathedral acoustics are basic to the 'other-worldly' atmosphere.

The Christian community in Rome was established during the reign of the Emperor Claudius (41–54 A.D.). Peter died in Rome in A.D. 64, with other Christians accused by Nero of the burning of Rome. The disciples of Christ, who established Christianity in Rome, certainly brought with them sacred songs they had sung in Israel. There is biblical evidence that they sang such songs. The Gospel according to St. Matthew, Chapter 26, verse 30 states: 'And when they had sung an hymn, they went out into the mount of Olives.' The early missions of Peter and Paul in Rome indicate the duality of culture which influenced the development of plainsong: Peter was an untutored Hebrew; Paul was 'Hebrew of Hebrews' but a citizen of Tarsus and culturally a Stoic Greek. Modern authorities such as Gastoué, Idelsohn, Ursprung and Peter Wagner, have acknowledged the influence of both Hebrew and Graeco-Roman music on plainsong. A comparison of the following examples will demonstrate this point.

Other names for plainsong are 'plainchant' or 'Gregorian chant.' Pope Gregory I (Gregory the Great, 504–604) was the first monk to become pope (590). His mentor was St. Benedict (480–544), who, like some European Buddha, renounced his

PLAINSONG

early masochism for a life of action. His political influence was enormous, particularly as mediator between Goths and Italians. From Benedict, Gregory learned organization. Gregory was the first to quell the dissident churches. He ruled Rome like a monarch (his Emperor was Chosroes II and the Lombards were dominant in Italy). He needed to exercise such authority, for A.D. 590, the year in which he was elected to the See, was also the year when plague raged in Rome. Gregory instigated missions, particularly to Britain, and he imposed Benedictine rule upon Latin monasticism. As a direct result of Gregory's missionary zeal, the venerable Bede (673-735), the monk of Jarrow on Tyne, became the foremost encyclopaedist of his age. It is from his reckoning of history from the birth of Christ that Christian chronology was accepted in Europe. The venerable Bede stated that he derived 'from the pupils of Blessed Pope Gregory ... his knowledge of the Roman Chant'. Gregory was responsible for putting the music of the Church of Rome into order by prescribing the modes (scales) to be used and by assembling the extensive collection of ancient ecclesiastic compositions known as Gregorian Music. The modes were inherited from Greek music (cf. Chapter 3) but renamed. The following list explains this:

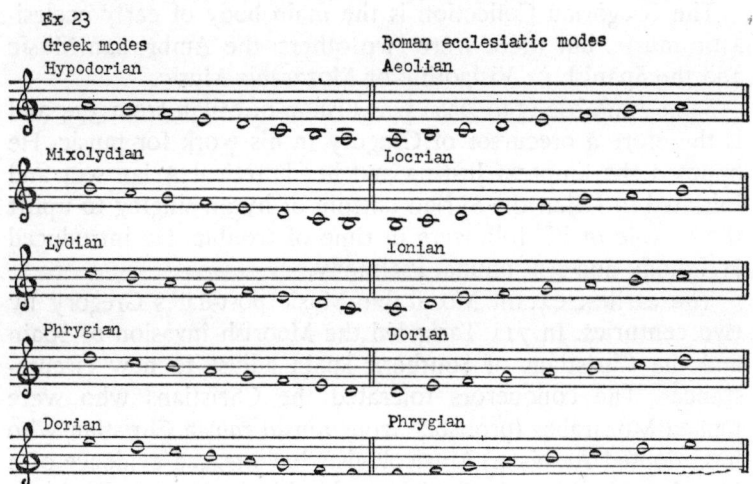

(The Locrian mode was rejected, as it was difficult to sing)

Gregorian Music has two divisions: the Mass or Missal, and the daily Hours of Divine Service or Breviary.

The Missal comprises over 600 settings of scripture. At the beginning and end of the Mass, a psalm and antiphon were sung. Between the Epistle and the Gospel a Respond, called the Gradual, and an Alleluia were sung; at Easter an Alleluia replaced the Gradual; on penitential occasions a Tract superseded the Alleluia.

The Hours of Divine Service consisted of Roman antiphonal chants. An Antiphon is responsorial, which means it is a psalm sung by a solo voice (the priest) answered by the congregational refrain or by two alternating choirs.

Very probably a singing school (*Schola Cantorum*) was founded towards the end of the 4th century. So Gregory was a consummator.

The Gregorian Collection is the main body of early ecclesiastic music, but there were two others: the Ambrosian Music and the Spanish or Visigothic or Mozarabic Music.

Saint Ambrose (340-397) was Bishop of Milan from 374 and is therefore a precursor of Gregory in his work for music. He opposed the Empress Justina and her heretical Arian sect and initiated in Milan the Syrian custom of hymn singing to uplift the morale of his followers in time of trouble. He introduced Hymnody and Antiphonal Psalmody.

The earliest extant Mozarabic Music post-dates Gregory by two centuries. In 711 Tariq led the Moorish invasion of Spain and the Christians of Southern Spain adjust to new circumstances. The conquerors tolerated the Christians who were named Mozarabes (probably from *musta rab*, a Christian who has adopted Arabism.) Musicologists have traced evidence of a Moorish admixture in the Mozarabic Music, but much of it is similar to the Gregorian Music.

Russian chant developed in the Orthodox Church during

PLAINSONG 39

the reign of Prince Vladimir (c. 956-1015). This erstwhile pagan and plunderer, whose court numbered 800 concubines and numerous wives, fell under the sway of Constantinople, became a convert to Christianity, thus converting Russia in 988, married Princess Anna, sister of the Byzantine Emperor Basil II, and was ultimately canonized as Saint Vladimir. He appointed the Bulgarian Bishop Michael first Metropolitan of Russia, and Michael fostered Russian chant. Bulgaria has made significant contributions to Russian culture, not least in giving Russia her alphabet, the Cyrilic Slav script invented by the Bulgarian brothers Cyril and Methodius in 855. Russian chant is more repetitious, incantational, rhapsodic and emotional than Gregorian chant. Chaliapin made a memorable recording of it.

Plainsong grew from the dictates of what is singable. Its melody moves by steps. Leaps of a third (from, say 'doh' to 'me') are also found in plainsong. Larger leaps than a third are infrequent. Leaps of a fifth or sixth are even more infrequent. The melody usually moves by step within the leap, e.g.

Ex 24

The compass of the melody is generally restricted to an octave and this is rarely exceeded. Very occasionally the note B is flattened to make the melody more easily singable. The rhythm moves in equal note length but the phrases end on notes of double length. The word-setting is generally syllabic (one note per syllable) but sometimes contains expressive *melismata*, that is, several notes sung to one syllable. There is no regular beat. Accentuation is guided by the natural stress of the words, so the rhythm sometimes moves in two-note and sometimes in three-note groups.

Traditionally, plainsong is unaccompanied. In recent times a simple organ accompaniment sometimes supports it, but this, if necessary to assist the choir, needs to be done discreetly and always by using simple harmonies derived from the mode employed.

That the Church of Rome, despite vicissitudes, has preserved the tradition and practice of plainsong, is largely due to the restoration work of the monks of the Priory of Solesmes, a village of Western France on the banks of the Sarthe. Three generations of Solesmes monks have patiently worked on ancient manuscripts: Dom Prosper Gueranger (1805–75); his pupil, Dom Joseph Pothier (1835–1923); and *his* pupil Dom André Mocquereau (1849–1930). (The notation of plainsong is treated in Chapter 6.)

Allusions to plainsong occasionally may be found in the non-ecclesiastic media of chamber music and symphonic music, as in the Lydian movement of Beethoven's String Quartet in A minor, op. 132, and Respighi's *Concerto Gregoriano* for violin and orchestra. Plainsong has understandably exercised a far-reaching influence on Italian vocal and operatic music, in the present century most notably in the cases of Pizzetti and Dallapiccola.

5 The Troubadours

Costumes of troubadours are familiar as they are depicted in the illuminated capitals of old writings on vellum. Some of us, while in the south of France, may have walked the roads that the wandering singers trod in the Middle Ages. The name 'troubadour' will suggest songs of knights and ladies to many. Few will realize that there is a deal more to it than this, and the troubadours of Provence really represented a protest movement against the orthodoxy of the Church of Rome. This protest began with the *goliards*, students in minor ecclesiastic orders who wandered over Western Europe between the 10th and 13th centuries. They derived their name from the probably mythical 'Bishop Golias', their patron. Their anti-clerical songs were in Latin. They were probably of the type that Medieval scholars called *conductus* or *conductum*, music originally sung when the officiating priest was processionally 'conducted' from vestry to altar or from chancel to nave. The melodies of popular songs may have been used for this purpose. Later the goliards would satirise the *conductus*, and, later still (in the 13th century) the *conductus* was accompanied by descant. Because the goliards satirised the Church, they were denied the 'privileges of the clergy'. Through their travels they began to bring dissension to Provence. The troubadours developed this dissension.

Troubadourism was the musical movement of the Albigenses. This word 'Albigenses' was the name given to the heretics of southern France in the 12th and 13th centuries. It was used by the chronicler Geoffrey de Vigeois in 1181. 'Albigenses' refers to Albi (the ancient Albiga), though it would have been more exact to locate the heretical centre at Toulose. The heresy was brought to Provence through trade routes from Bulgaria. Even within orthodoxy, the Bulgarians had pioneered progressive movements, as when the brothers Cyril and Methodius successfully petitioned the Pope for worship in the vernacular Bulgarian instead of Latin (a 9th century innovation which was eleven centuries in advance of the ecumenical reforms of 20th century Rome!) In 10th century Thracian Bulgaria, Bogomilism sprang up, named after its founder. It spread to other Balkan countries and to France and Italy. It was essentially a dualistic religious view of the world, stressing the conflict between good and evil in nature, but also embodying rationalistic social teaching opposed to feudal oppression. The Bogomils saw the established Church as worldly and Satanic. They favoured a return to the earliest forms of Christianity, from which they held Rome to have departed. The Provençal Catharists, who were influenced by the Bogomils, were highly respected as *bons hommes* by the people of Provence and protected by its Princes. Troubadour music grew out of this ethos.

The troubadours were the minstrels of southern France. Their counterparts in northern France were called 'trouvères'. The language of the troubadours was *langue d'oc*, an amalgam of Midi dialects. The language of the trouvères was *langue l'oil*, the origin of modern French. The names 'troubadour' and 'trouvère' derived either from the Latin *tropus*, the 8th or 9th century Byzantine florid interpolation or tail-piece to the Church chant, or from *trobar*, meaning to find or invent (the medieval Scottish equivalent was *makar*, poet or maker of verse.) Troubadour music was unaccompanied song, often improvised and therefore rhythmically free. Ezra Pound, in his essay 'Troubadours – their sorts and conditions', finds their tunes 'perhaps a little Oriental in feeling, and it is likely that the spirit of Sufism is not wholly absent from their content.' This may well have been the Bulgarian influence, for Bulgaria is a cultural bridge between East and West. The following Provençal May Day Song by Rambaut de Vaqueiras (d. 1207) has a final melismatic cadence very like Bulgarian song:

THE TROUBADOURS 43

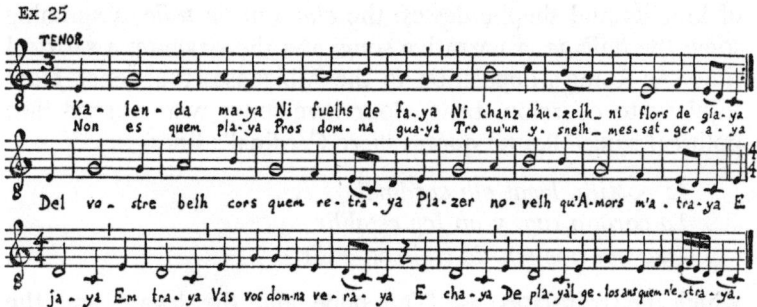

Troubadours and trouvères were active from the middle of the 11th century till the end of the 13th century; troubadours mainly in the first half of that period, trouvères mainly in the second half. Troubadourism spread from southern to northern France through the intermingling during the crusades. Pope Urban proclaimed the first Crusade in 1095 and Richard the Lion Heart himself (d. 1199) was a troubadour. Another factor in the development of trouverism was that Eleanor of Aquitaine (c. 1122–1204) was a patroness of troubadours, some of whom she called to service in northern France.

The troubadour, Folquet de Marseilles (d. 1231) declared: 'a verse without music – a mill without water'. Some scholars aver that the troubadours composed exclusively in triple time – three beats to a bar or measure, which they varied by an ingenious system of rhythmic modes.

Troubadour song derived from four basic types, three of them liturgical: the litany, the ecclesiastic sequence (a melismatic interpolation in the Mass), the hymn and the roundel (possibly a secular dance or possibly a carol). From these four basic types sprang many song forms, replete with ingenious structural devices, both in versification and in melody. The ecclesiastic Dorian and Mixolydian modes were favoured. The *chanson de geste* was an epic chronicle in song, describing the deeds of Charlemagne, Roland or Huon de Bordeaux. Short syllabic phrases were repeated but it was not strophic or stanzaic. These songs were improvised and passed on by oral tradition; few were written down. The *chante-fable* was part verse, part prose. The *canso* was a love song; the *tenso* a debating song; the *alba*, a dawn song; the *pastourelle*, a song of knights and shepherdesses; the *chanson de toile*, a spinning song; the *ballade*, a narrative song; and the *sirvente*, a satirical song. As Rome's opposition to the Albigenses toughened from cajolery to coercion, troubadour love songs were turned into political songs. Pound quotes Piere Cardinal's lines

> *Li postilh, legat elh cardinal*
> *La cordon tug, y an fag establir*
> *Que qui nos pot de traisson esdir,*

which he translates as, 'The pope and the legate and the cardinal have twisted such a cord that they have brought things to such a pass that no one can escape committing treachery'.

When the anti-heretical decisions of the Council of Tours (1163) and the Ecumenical Lateran Council (1179) had but little effect on the Albigenses, Innocent III resolved to suppress them. Rome had to contend not only with the heretics, but with the Provençal nobles who protected them and the populace who revered them. In 1204 Innocent III suspended the authority of the bishops of the south of France. Peter of Castelnau excommunicated Raymond VI, Count of Toulouse, in 1207. The Provençal nobles responded by murdering him in 1209. Innocent III then commanded the Cistercians to preach crusade against the Albigenses. This crusade, which pitted northern against southern France, raged for 20 years, and ended in the Treaty of Paris in 1229 and in the ruin of the brilliant Provençal civilization. The celebrated troubadors, who might otherwise have been as well known and loved as later composers, are now only names in history books, except for students interested enough to track down old manuscripts: such names as Guilhem IX, Count of Poitiers and Duke of Aquitaine (c. 1087–1127); Bernart de Ventadorn or Ventadour (d. 1195); Guirant de Bornelh (d.c. 1220); and Guirant Riquier (13th century).

As northern France was victorious over the south, the northern trouvères lingered on: such men as Blondel de Nesle (fl. early 13th century); Thibaut IV, Count of Champagne and King of Navarre (1201–53); Moniot d'Arras, founder of a 13th century *puy* (academy) at Arras, a century before it produced its tapestries; and Adam de la Halle (c. 1230–1288), composer of choral as well as solo vocal music and whose work numbers the dramatic pastoral, *Li Gieus* (*Le Jeu*) *de Robin et Marion*, the first *opera comique* (premiered at the French Court in Naples in 1275 or 1285). The following quotation from a song of Thibaut IV mirrors only too well his tragic times:

Ex 26

Pour ce___ se d'a - mer me___ dueil Si i ai___ je___ argnt con - fort

A lower order of troubadour was the *jongleur* (from whom the modern word 'juggler' may derive). The jongleur was sometimes an assistant to a troubadour, sometimes playing introductions, interludes or tail-pieces to the troubadour's unaccompanied song. Troubadours served in the castles; contrary to popular fallacy, they weren't mendicant minstrels. The wanderers were the jongleurs, who sometimes even had performing bears. They were versatile instrumentalists, performing on the vièle (medieval fiddle), lute, guitar, harp or small portative organ. As vagabonds, difficult to track down, they gave vent to anti-clerical satire even more freely than the troubadours did.

After the annulment of Eleanor of Aquitaine's marriage to Louis VII of France in 1152, she married Henry of Anjou, founder of the Angevin lineage of English Kings. Eleanor brought troubadourism to England, but it did not flourish there.

Troubadourism also found its way into Spain. Alfonso X, *el Sabio* ('the Wise'), King of Castile and Leon (1252–84), compiled the *Cantigas de Santa Maria* (over 400 songs). Guirant de Bornelh was active in Spain and Guirant Riquier visited Alfonso's court. Seven *canciones* of the jongleur Martin Codex also survive.

In 1156 Frederick Barbarossa, the first Hohenstaufen to be Emperor of the Holy Roman Empire, married Beatrix of Burgundy. Guiot de Provins, troubadour, was in her entourage. Thus began the influence of French song on Germany, though before that the *Gaukler* (or *fahrende Sänger*), the German jongleurs had wandered the roads along the Rhine. The *Minnesinger* (*Minne* = chivalrous love), mostly nobles, were active in Bavaria and Austria in the 12th and 13th centuries. Their songs took the form of *Lied* (= Provençal *canso*); Tagelied (= *alba*); Leich (= lai or lay); and the *Spruch* (= *tenso* or proverb). Chief among the Minnesingers was Walther von der Vogelweide (c. 1160–1228). Here is the opening of his *Palastinalied* of 1228:

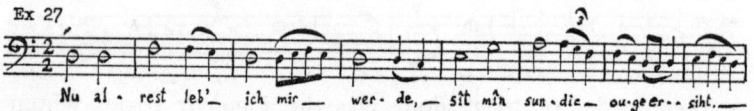

The *Meistersingers* (mastersingers) were a later and more organized group related to the Minnesingers. They organized themselves into guilds of poet-composers. Their first guild was founded by Heinrich von Meissen (named Frauenlob) in Mainz in 1311. In a sense this was the first Musicians' Union. As in the crafts, the guild members graduated through the stages of *Schuler* (apprentice), *Schulfreund* (assistant in a school), *Sanger* (singer), *Dichter* (poet), and *Meister* (master). The most famous Meister was Hans Sachs (1494–1576) who was, of course, portrayed by Wagner in his opera *Die Meistersinger*. Here is Sachs's *May Day Song* of 1562:

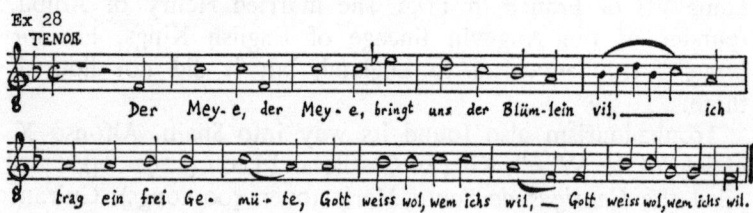

The Mastersinger songs were melodically simpler than those of the troubadours, but were ingenious in metre and rhyme. Sachs was a contemporary of Luther. In 16th century Germany, power was shifting from the princes to the burghers and artisans, who were beginning to assert themselves. The Mastersingers came from the ranks of the ascendent middle class.

This period, encompassing the 11th–13th centuries, is no mere feminolatry of song but the first flowering of European secular melody. For the first time in Europe, melody was brought out from the incense-laden cathedral atmosphere of the mysticism of divinity into the Maytime of man's dawning consciousness of his own humanity.

POSTSCRIPT: The Vikings were the troubadours of the seas. Old ballads such as *Lord Brand*, *The Maid Freed from the Gallows* and *The Two Sisters*, which have been unearthed in the current folk revival, often have Viking origin. *The Maid Freed from the Gallows* exists in variants from Estonia, the Faroes, Russia, Sicily and Sweden. Ethnomusicologists trace this ballad back through an ancient Yorkshire version to a 9th century Irish folk tale, *The Distressed Handmaid*. Thus, this song was created in Dublin (which was founded by Vikings in the 9th century) and reappeared in York (a 10th century Viking capital), in Novgorod and Kiev (10th century Viking strongholds), in Scandinavia (the Vikings' home), Estonia (dominated by Vikings), the Faroes (settled by Vikings) and Sicily (ruled in the 12th century by the Norman descendants of the Vikings). Probably such ballads ultimately originated in Norse culture of the previous millenium. The Danish Bronze Age 'Lur' (c. 800 B.C.), examples of which have been disinterred by archeologists, reproduced an animal horn in bronze. It is in a contorted 'S' shape, with a trombone-like mouthpiece and a large ornamental disc at the other end. Lurs have been found in pairs. This may indicate that the Ur-Norsemen employed two-part harmony, which is still found in the two-part folk songs of Iceland.

6 Gothic Music

The term 'Gothic', whether used of architecture or music, is a misnomer, but as it has long been common usage, so we retain it. It was first employed at the end of the 17th century or beginning of the 18th. The diarist John Evelyn used it in 1702. He maintained that the Goths (whom he wrongly ejuated with the Vandals – they were related but not the same) demolished the classical architecture of antiquity and 'introduced their own licentious style now called modern or Gothic'. So, like so much of man's terminology, it doesn't mean what it implies. Gothic architecture or Gothic music are *not* arts of the Goths.

One of the most graphic symbols of the Gothic impulse is seen in Rodin's sculpture entitled La Cathèdrale. It shows praying hands which symbolize the spire of a church.

The spire was introduced into Gothic architecture by elongating the steep roof of Romanesque towers, and the Romanesque style may have acquired the steep roof from the pointed arch and domes of Arabic mosques. The Gothic spirit animated music from the 13th to 17th centuries, that is, over a longer period than it prevailed in architecture. And the spire – or that sculpture of Rodin's of the praying hands – epitomises mankind's aspiring spirit during this period. The 13th century gave birth to Roger Bacon, a prophet of experimental science, to Duns Scotus, a philosopher who applied dialectics to Franciscanism; it was the age of Marco Polo's travels. Mankind was moving. The 14th century witnessed the Jacquerie, the French peasant uprising of 1358; the English Peasant Revolt followed in 1381. Dante and Chaucer wrote in

GOTHIC MUSIC

their own languages, Italian and English, the language of the people; not in Latin, the language of the scholars. The 15th century brought the first printed books (Coster of Haarlem); the Portuguese discovered Cape Verde, Diaz rounded the Cape of Good Hope, Columbus crossed the Atlantic to America. In 1519 Leonardo died and Magellan set sail on a voyage round the world. Those are only a few indications of what the Gothic spirit was. It was the spirit that thrust up the spires of the great Cathedrals of Notre Dame de Paris, Chartres and Amiens.

How did this impulse to progress express itself in music? It expressed itself by taking on a new dimension. Instead of the single line of plainsong or troubadour song, it became a music of many voices. Just as Gothic architecture, beginning in the 11th and 12th centuries, raised spiring cathedrals over north-west Europe, Gothic music, beginning a little later, in the 13th century, raised the single dimension of melody to 'three-dimensional' polyphony. There evolved a music of interlacing voices, like the intertwining of tree-branches in north-west European forests, or like the vistas of vaulted arches in stone-chiselled filigree, one seen through another, in the Gothic cathedrals. And with the new era there was a geographic shift of the cultural centre. At the time of Gregory I the focal point was Rome; when it moved to Provence, with the advent of the troubadours; now the centres were Britain, northern France and Scandinavia.

This branching-out of music from unaccompanied melody to many melodies accompanying each other, was no sudden happening. It evolved over a long period. We found earlier in this book that the octave and/or the fifth were the harmonies of antiquity and may still be heard in bagpipe music. The octave and fifth ('do' and its higher 'so') or octave and fourth ('do' and its lower 'so') are the basic pitch differentials between human voices. The soprano is naturally pitched an octave above the tenor; the contralto an octave above the bass. The soprano is also a fifth above the contralto; the tenor a fifth above the bass; and the contralto is a fourth above the tenor. These relationships determined the role of tonic/dominant ('doh' to 'soh') harmonic functions which, later, were important in the baroque fugue and the classical sonata. Primitive man's instinct to imitate would presumably have led to attempts at unison singing. But as man's experience increased and his intelligence sharpened through adaptation to environment, the person with the lower voice would do what the bright boy with a broken voice does in classroom singing: he would drop his voice in a lower pitch instead of straining on high notes. One may conjecture that this is how primitive harmony evolved.

There are two kinds of primitive harmony: that in fourths or fifths, called *organum*, and that in thirds or sixths, called *gymel* (from the Latin *gemellum*, meaning 'twin song', from *gemini*, the heavenly twins). Generally speaking, organum preceded gymel chronologically. Indeed, among contemporary aborigines one still hears a form of organum in their harmonized songs. In 1963 I adjudicated a children's choir competition at the Bantu location of Nyanga, Cape Town. They sang Scottish folksongs arranged by Sir Hugh Roberton. (A Bantu clergyman had visited Scotland and had returned with a batch of these arrangements.) Where the music was printed in consecutive thirds (gymel), the children simply sang in consecutive fourths (organum). They were translating the music into their own vernacular. And not only aborigines sing in organum in the 20th century, but also civilized people who, because of their geographic position, have been isolated. For instance there are modern Icelandic student songs (*Tvi söngvar*/two-part songs) which harmonize in fifths, such as this one:

Ex 29

On the other hand, the Welsh, as a nation, are such fine natural singers that they often spontaneously harmonize in thirds (gymel); and it may be that, in early Celtic history, they harmonized in thirds instead of fourths. Harmonization in *seconds* is a characteristic feature of some Slav folk-song, particularly Bulgarian; but it is thought that this practice resulted from the singers' taking account of the acoustic phenomenon that dissonance travels further in the open air than consonance. But through centuries of Bulgarian folk harmonization, the singers do not feel the interval of the second (which sounds to genteel western ears like two rival motor car horns!) to be dissonant.

Hucbald, the learned monk (c. 840-930), in his treatise, *De harmonica institutione*, gives an illustration of organum which, transcribed into modern notation reads:

Ex 30

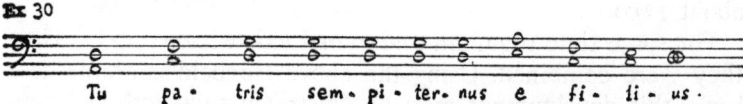

The higher voice was called the *vox principalis*, the lower the *vox organalis*. The organ probably assisted the choir in keeping to the lower part.

In organum, the lower voice repeats the pattern of the upper, at the interval of a fourth below (as in ex. 30) or a fifth above, when the upper voice repeats the lower:

Ex 31

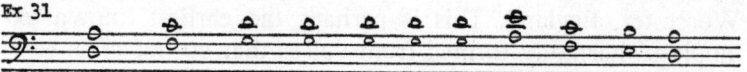

They move in the same direction (the technical term for this is 'similar motion'). When the two parts move in *opposite* direction ('contrary motion') and overlap, the intervals still being fourths (or occasionally a fifth or unison), we have a development of primitive organum into elementary counterpoint. Here is an example from Coussemaker's *Histoire de l'harmonie au moyen age*:

Ex 32

The following is an example of gymel, from a short piece for three instruments by Guilelmus Monachus (c. 1450, probably English); the gymel is the upper two parts:

Ex 33

But gymel was in use certainly in the early 13th century, if not before. The English gymel, *Foweles in the Frith*, dates from about 1250.

For some time organum and gymel existed separately. Then they were combined. Using the above Hucbald example as a basis, this development may be illustrated succinctly:

Ex 34   a) Organum   b) Gymel   a) and b) combined

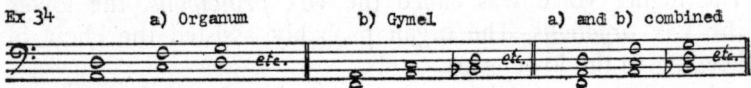

For some time music consisted of bare organum and full harmony juxtaposed, as in *Beata Viscera*, an anonymous 3-part vocal conductus found in a 13th century MS at Worcester, England. This is perhaps the earliest known example of harmony formed from voices that do not cross each other:

Ex 35

The influence of monody, the single-line melody of plainsong and troubador song, was still strong enough to suggest that one strand of melody, in such music as our last example, should be emphasised more than the others. So the question arises of where the main tune lies. The musicologist Manfred Bukofzer suggests that medieval English music has the main melody in the *lowest* part whereas Continental music of the period has the main melody in the *highest* part. The part or parts added to the main tune is called *faburden(s)* or *fauxbourdon(s)*, i.e. the false tune(s). The main tune was called the *cantus fermus*, or holding part, i.e. the part that held the main tune. The voice that sang the *cantus fermus* was generally the tenor. The word 'tenor' derives from the verb *tenere*, which also means 'to hold'. So the tenor part was one that held the main tune or that carried the burden of the song.

England was certainly ahead of the Continent in the practice of gymel. An example is the 12th century Hymn of St. Magnus from Kirkwall Cathedral, Orkney. The famous English round, the so-called Reading Rota, *Sumer is icumen in* (Harley MS 978, British Museum) is an example of developed gymel, for this four-part canon over a two-part ground bass of a repeated phrase (named *pes* in the MS) moves mainly in thirds and sixths.

For long this round was thought to date from c. 1240, but Bukofzer has brought forward circumstantial evidence suggesting the date c. 1310. This round sounds like folk-polyphony. Perhaps it is an ecclesiastic transcription of original folk material; perhaps it may even be of Celtic origin, remembering the Welsh flair for gymel.

It may be as well to add a parenthisis here about the device of canon. The word means 'law', i.e. music incorporating a law of how the different strands of melody will move in relation to each other. A graphic analogy is a walking person and his shadow. The person is like the tune; the shadow is like the canonic imitation of the tune which follows the first tune. A canon which is repeated over and over, or round and round again, is called a round (rota).

Sumer is icumen in is not unique, as it was thought to be, though it is more developed than anything of its time. Perhaps other similar music existed but was suppressed by the Church or lost. Embryonic canon is found in the works of the Notre Dame school.

Pope Alexander III laid the cornerstone of Notre Dame Cathedral in 1163 and it was completed 60 years later, though various modifications were made down to the 14th century. The changes of style built into the great cathedrals have their counterpart in music's changes of style. This overlapping of periods and styles is difficult to convey in separate chapters of a book. One has not only to 'read between the lines' but to 'read between the chapters'. For instance in the mid-12th century, when the Magister Leoninus was *organista* (composer of *organa* – pl. of organum) and maitre de chapelle at Beate Mariae Virginus (which, rebuilt, became Notre Dame) the troubadours were active in southern France. Leoninus represented a development of ecclesiastic music; the troubadours a development of secular music. Leonin (a diminution of Leo) took two-part organum a step further by decorating one part in broad melodic sequences (repeated patterns). His successor Perotinus Magnus (Perotin the Great or – rather oddly – Little Pierre the Great), active towards the end of the 12th century, extended Leonin's two and occasional three-part compositions to four parts. But even in four parts, the harmony of the school of Notre Dame remained basically that of organum, that is, mainly the so-called 'perfect' intervals of unison, octave, fourth and fifth. These are the sonorities which sound best in the acoustics of the wide spaces of cathedral architecture. There is a certain relationship between the solid yet spacious basic sound of this music and the solid, spacious edifices in stone; and the melodic embroidery which was introduced above the basic harmony was a sonal analogy to the coloured glass windows which relieved the architectural austerity and illumined the spaciousness.

As music became polyphonic, it became necessary to write it down in order to ensure ensemble. Boethius (c. 475–524 or 525), an Italian scholar-composer who studied in his native Rome and in Athens, developed the Greek alphabetic music notation in Italy. About the 7th century a system of *neums* or *neumes* (lozenge-shaped signs) was gradually introduced from Aquitaine for the notation of plainsong. A single line indicated the pitch of the principal note. Guido d'Arezzo

GOTHIC MUSIC 55

(c. 990–1050), a Benedictine pedagogue, invented mnemonic systems of sol-fa and hand-signs to aid sight singing (the 'Guidonian hand'). He gave Latin capitals to the notes, beginning with G 𝄢 from which derived the name *gamut* (the complete scale) and later the G or treble clef. Guido added a second line to notation: a yellow line for C, a red one for F; and, if a B flat was needed to make the vocally difficult interval F-B singable, he added a third line, a green one for this flattened note. These coloured MS became characteristically Italian. So Guido is sometimes credited with the invention of the stave, that 'five-barred gate' (Percy Scholes's apt analogy) on which we write notes in modern notation, and which, if we understand it, opens to the broad fields of music.

Notation is a short-cut to understanding music. If you can't read music, you have to take a long way round to get to an understanding of it. That 'long way round' is repeated listening. Really to know a piece of music, you've got to be able to remember early sections of it and relate them to the later sections. A musically illiterate person can only do that after repeated hearings. Musical literacy enables comprehension of the kind you have when you stand before a painting and take it in at one glance (even if it's a long glance).

Franco of Cologne (late 12th century) developed Guidonian notation much further. In his *Ars cantus mensurabilis* he codified rhythmically measured music. With him music notation begins to look much more modern than the neums. His vocabulary of notes is:

Ex 37

double long	long	breve	semibreve
▐	▐	■	◆

As is usual in history, mankind got things wrong. The clear Franconian notation, which differentiated between long and short notes, got turned upside down after the Renaissance, so that the longest note in modern notation is now paradoxically called the *breve* (brief)! Franconian notation employed time signatures: a circle (symbol of God without beginning or end) indicated triple time (symbol of the Trinity); a broken circle indicated duple time.

Such were the problems of ensemble in polyphonic music that a host of theorists applied themselves to solving them: two Englishmen, Walter Odington (13th century) and Robert de Handlo (14th century); Johannes de Muris (14th century French); and two 15th century Italians, Franchinus Gaforius and Prosdocimus de Beldemandis. (The 20th century English composer Peter Warlock baffled people by using Prosdocimus's grandiloquent name as a pseudonym!)

Instead of wading through a mass of abstruse material about these theorists, it is more to the point to give a few of the terms which they used. *Musica plana* was music in free rhythm, i.e. not measured music; it is a general term for plainsong and organum. *Musica mensurata* was literally, 'measured music' in a system of notation expressing relative duration of rhythm and position of pitch. *Musica figurata* added decorative melodic sequences to a background of organum. *Musica ficta* (or *falsa*) was the system of adding flats or sharps (semitonal lowering or raising of pitch) to facilitate polyphonic singing; this gradually extended the seven-note pitch vocabulary of Guidonian *musica vera* ('true music') to the twelve notes of the chromatic scale, all of which Prosdocimus lists, though he says that A sharp and D sharp were rarely employed.

Those terms cover techniques and niceties of style. There were other, broader terms, for example *ars antiqua* and *ars nova*. Some modern writers use the term *ars antiqua* to cover the music of Leonin and Perotin, but 14th century writers meant by it the style of the late 13th century motet, explained later. *Ars nova* was the title of Philippe de Vitri's 14th century treatise and has been loosely applied to the music of his time. *Ars antiqua* lingered on, however, after the new style was established. *Ars antiqua* included organum, conductus (already explained), motet and cantilena. *Ars nova* concentrated on and developed the last two, tending to abandon organum and the conductus. *Ars antiqua* employed only triple rhythm in one of the six rhythmic modes founded on the metrical feet of classical poetry. *Ars nova* employed binary rhythm also, im-

GOTHIC MUSIC 57

porting it into France through the rhythmic influence of Italian folk-music, probably introduced into France with the transference of the Papal See from Rome to Avignon in 1309.

When musicians speak of the motet, they are generally referring to Palestrina or Bach, but the 13th century motet was different from either of those. The word motet derived either from *motulus* which suggests *modulus* (melody) or from the Italian *motetto* (a little motto) and the French *mot* (word), with reference to the 'motto' around which other texts were woven. The 13th century motet had a multiplicity of text and, taking a pre-existent tenor melody containing repeated patterns, wound round it other voices with occasional repeated patterns in the melody. The second voice was called the *motetus*; the third, the *triplum*. These features were developed further in the 14th century motet, the repeated rhythmic patterns in the tenor being called *taleae* (literally 'cuttings' i.e. sections 'cut to measure' the composition as it were); the melodic sequences being called *colores*.

The *cantilenae* were polyphonic settings of trouvère dance-songs with refrains, the *rondeaux* and *ballades*. This extension of trouvère song was not as great a step as may at first appear, because the refrains of those songs were traditionally sung by chorus after the verses of solo singing. Unlike the motet, all voices in the cantilena had the same text.

De Vitri (1291–1351) was born in the district of Champagne, in a town now named after him, and died at Meaux, where he was Bishop. He was composer, poet, theorist and diplomat. The Italian poet Petrarch praised his music, poetry and inquiring spirit. Isorhythm (identical patterns of rhythm superimposed on variable melody) unified the de Vitri motets, which are indeed known as 'isorhythmic motets'.

Born in the same district of Champagne as de Vitri was Guillaume de Machaut (c. 1300–1377), who was probably the greatest composer of the 14th century. He became a priest early in life and then secretary to king John of Bohemia, Duke of Luxembourg, and finally became Canon of Rheims. He was a mundane ecclesiastic, in which he resembled an earlier type of Franz Liszt. In old age he conducted a love affair by correspondence with a certain Peronne, which he set to music.

He was a prolific composer and also a poet, some of whose lines were paraphrased by Chaucer. He wrote 18 lays or *lais*, 16 of which are monodic, like the last late flowering of trouvère-song. Their form generally consists of 12 strophes (stanzas), the first and last identical in poem and music, with different words and melody for each of the intervening 10 strophes. He is versatile: some of his tunes are simple, others are ornamented. There was a dichotomy in his style: he embraced innovation but also had nostalgia for the age of chivalry. His 25 *chansons balladées* harks back to the trouvère songs, but, unlike them, employs binary rhythm. He also favours syncopation (a reshuffling of strong and weak beats) which gives his music vivacity, as in his *Douce dame jolie*:

Ex 38

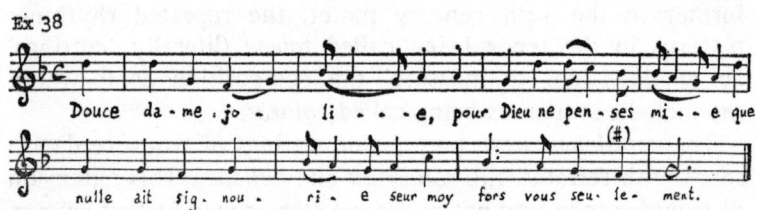

His 21 *rondeaux* in two, three and four parts are full of sophisticated polyphony. One of them, *Ma fin est mon commencement*, is (appropriately in relation to the content of the text) a *cancrizans* (crab) canon; that is, it sets against a tune a version of itself that goes backwards. As so often in terminology, this word 'cancrizans' is a misnomer, for, meaning 'crab' as it does, its use overlooks the fact that a crab moves sideways, not backwards. But the point is that Machaut makes a playful, delightful piece out of this idea. Without the delight, the ingenuity would be worth nothing. The ingenuity itself looks forward to the ingenuity that was so typical of the later Flemish school. Of his 42 *ballades notées* (*notées* implying 'set to music', to differentiate them from his purely poetic ballades) one is monodic; the rest polyphonic. He also wrote 23 isorhythmic motets. His Mass (*Messe Notre Dame*) is the first known complete polyphonic setting achieved by one composer. An *Ite missa est* is added to the usual five sections. The *Gloria* and *Credo* are traditionally set to plainsong to be sung by the celebrant. The whole Mass is unified by a recurrent motive   Ex 39

which engenders canonic imitation, fugal entries and countermelodies. He displays dramatic instinct in employing dissonance on the word *Crucifixus*, but the Mass is generally austere in effect.

But liturgical music was only a small part of Machaut's output. Most of his music is secular. This fact may relate to the Papal Bull of John XXII (1324–5) at Avignon, proscribing nearly all polyphony from the church service but insisting on plainsong.

If Machaut was the greatest composer of the 14th century, the Englishman John Dunstable (c. 1370–1453) was the greatest of the 15th. His epitaph, in St. Stephen's Walbrook, tells us that he was also an astronomer and mathematician. Yet fewer than 60 compositions are preserved of this master musician who strongly influenced his continental contemporaries. But he was also modest enough to be influenced by such a younger composer as Dufay. Indeed, the relationship between these two men has been compared to that between Haydn and Mozart. To the styles and forms we have already considered, Dunstable added the declamation motet and the double-structure style. His declamation motet, unlike the Continental motet, is not based on a traditional tenor melody but entirely on original material or a traditional melody varied ('colored') beyond recognition. The declamation of the text dictates the musical rhythm, all the parts move chordally, which emphasizes the 'declamatory' effect, and all the parts are of equal importance. While the declamation motet uses no recognizably traditional melodic material, the double-structure style employs *two* traditional melodies simultaneously.

A *Gloria* and *Credo* of Dunstable (edition *Denkmaler der Tonkunst in Oesterreich* XXXI, p. 114 ff.) are both based on the same tenor, which shows how Dunstable developed Machaut's attempts at unificationn of the movements of the Mass.

Between 1423–35 Dunstable visited the Court of Burgundy as a member of the retinue of the Duke of Bedford, the Regent of France under whom, incidentally, Joan of Arc was burned at the stake. The French poet, Martin le Franc, in his poem *Le Champion des Dames* (c. 1440) dedicated to the Duke of Burgundy, attests to Dunstable's influence on the Burgundian composers Dufay and Binchois:

> The English guise they wear with grace,
> They follow Dunstable aright,
> And thereby have they learned apace
> To make their music gay and bright.

Dunstable certainly enriched Continental harmony by his six-part *O rosa bella*, which is unlike any other work of its period. It begins:

and contains passages of expressive dissonance such as this:

Instrumental music began to be developed also during the Gothic period. The Louvre has an ivory lute dating from 968. Among instruments depicted in Medieval vellums are: the monochord, used for pedagogic purposes by Guido d'Arezzo; the lute-shaped, three or five-string rebec, played with a bow and called *gigue* in France and *Geige* in Germany; viols; cymbals, castanets, tambourines, single bells and sets of small bell-chimes; flutes, recorders and reed instruments such as the shawm (an early bass oboe); trumpets, horns and bagpipes.

The most significant development in medieval instrument building was the addition of the keyboard to the organ in the 13th century. Previously, pieces of wood were pulled out to allow air in the pipes or reinserted to prevent the passage of air. Obviously, only slowish music could be performed like this. The keyboard increased the speed and intricacy of organ music. It also adapted organs to transport. The 'positive' organ had to be set down; the 'portative' could be carried and played in processions. The portative organ was sometimes called the *regal*. This did not imply 'royal' but derived from the Latin *regula* ('rule'), implying that it was used to 'rule' or 'regulate' the chanting of the monks.

Music of the Gothic period is some of the richest. Though it contained many future ideas in embryo, it should be appreciated as music in its own right, with splendours just as refulgent as later music.

7 Flemish Music

The earliest Netherland charters date from the 12th century. A number of semi-independent feudatories grew up in the feudal state, the most flourishing in Flanders – Ghent, Bruges and Ypres, which became large industrial towns, Bruges being connected with the sea, with its port of Sluis, the mart of world trade. Guilds were organized among weavers (the most powerful), fullers, dyers, smiths, leather workers, brewers, butchers and bakers. United, they rebelled against the *leliaerts* (patricians). The battle of Courtrai (1302) felled French chivalry. After a century, though, municipal jealousies made the Netherlands pregnable. Gradually during the 15th century, by royal marriage, money, treachery or force, the Netherlands fell under Burgundian dominion. By 1473 Charles the Bold dominated the Netherlands.

So it was that the Burgundian composers Dufay and Binchois (already mentioned towards the end of the previous chapter) became the leaders of the first Netherland school of composers, which more properly should be called the Franco-Flemish school.

Guillaume Dufay (c. 1400–74) was a chorister in Cambrai Cathedral, and at 16 wrote an epithalamium for Carlo Malates and Vittoria di Lorenzo Colonna, sang in the Papal Choir in Rome 1428–37, and ended his days as canon of Cambrai and Mons. Apart from the Dunstable influence, his work shows Italian clarity. (Dunstable also set Italian, as in *O rosa bella*, but never visited Italy.)

Gilles Binchois (c. 1440–60) was first a soldier, then a priest at Mons, where he was a colleague of Dufay. He chiefly wrote secular music.

Both Dufay and Binchois developed the English faubourdon 'discant' style but put the *cantus fermus* in the top voice, whereas the English put it in the bottom part. Later this was introduced into England, where it really began and yet where it was hailed as an innovation!

One tradition avers that Binchois taught Johannes Okeghem (b. early 15th century – d.c. 1495), who was born in East Flanders, was a chorister in Antwerp in 1444, in the service of Duke Charles of Bourbon at Moulins, 1446–48, and about 1452 served the King of France. Louis XI appointed him treasurer of St. Martin's at Tours. He visited Spain in 1469.

Okeghem was the founder of the second or new Netherland school. He was a 'musician's musician'. The delight in contrapuntal detail displayed in his work could only be assimilated with study. His melodic writing employs a wide variety of ecclesiastic modes within one and the same composition, as in his *Missa cujusvis toni*, whereas his predecessors generally kept to one mode for one composition. He extended polyphonic writing from the former three-part norm to four-part, five-part and six-part writing and even produced a motet for 36 parts. His contrapuntal writing developed canon by augmentation, by diminution and inversion. In the chapter on Gothic music, canon was described as a tune with its shadow. Extending this metaphor, we might say that canon by augmentation is a tune with its lengthened shadow, i.e. the tune answered by itself in another voice but in longer notes. And we might say that canon by diminution is a tune with its foreshortened shadow, i.e. the tune answered by itself in another voice but in shorter notes. Canon by inversion (a tune answered by itself upside down) is a tune with its reflection (implied by the other name for it, 'mirror-canon'.)

The second Netherlands school revelled in the device of *ennime*, enigmatic or puzzle canons. The composer would simply write out the melody with some cryptogram, which, when solved, would indicate the solution of the canon, that is, the ratio of rhythm and of pitch at which the second voice would answer the first. This kind of intelligence-exercise has no intrinsic musicality and, if unenlivened by a musical idea, produces an effect of desiccated cerebralism, like some experimental music of the 20th century. But this fascination for device was very much part of the Netherlands during the 15th and 16th centuries. Another manifestation of it was the 'Chamber of Rhetoric' which every town of the Low Countries boasted at that time. This was a middle-class literary guild, a related form of organization to the trade guilds mentioned at the beginning of this chapter. Each Chamber had its own fanciful or heraldic title: 'The Alpha and Omega' at Ypres (founded 1398); the 'Violet' at Antwerp (1400); the 'Book' at Brussels (1401); the 'Marigold' at Gouda (1437); and the 'Eglantine' at Amsterdam, with its motto *In Liefde Bloeyende* ('Blossoming in Love') (1496). They held *landjuweelen*, tournaments of rhetoric, which offered rich prizes. Thousands of *literati* attended. The Chambers sent their members on horseback, in crimson mantles. Their literary productions were of a didactic cast, allegories and moral abstractions. This was the same ethos that lay behind the canonic music of Okeghem.

But the second Netherlands school also contained much expressive music. Jakob Obrecht (c. 1430–1505) who was born in Utrecht, where he was choirmaster at the Cathedral – as a boy Erasmus of Rotterdam was one of his scholars – and died in Ferrara, composed the first passion motet. This work is for four voices. The text is selected from the four Gospels and the work is in three sections, the first ending with Christ before Pilate, the second with his condemnation, the third with the crucifixion. Obrecht is more conservative than Okeghem in his employment of the modes: he keeps to the customary Ionian mode (the modern major scale); but his writing is genuinely felt.

Josquin des Prez (c. 1450–1521) was the greatest composer to bridge the 15th and 16th centuries. He was born probably at Conde in Hennegau. Josquin is the diminutive of Josse. He was a pupil of the Collegiate Church of St. Quentin and a student of Okeghem, who was a renowned teacher (a kind of 15th century Schoenberg, both in his interest in technical innovation and in his pedagogic ability). Josquin also came under the influence of Obrecht. In this way, he coalesced the two tributary streams of the second Netherland school, the technical expertise of Okeghem and the emotional range of

Obrecht; and brought the school to its full fruition. (This differentiation between Okeghem and Obrecht is a generalization; it neither implies that Okeghem was incapable of expression nor that Obrecht was technically limited.) Josquin was contemporary with Leonardo da Vinci and, like him, was a glory of the Renaissance. His corpus includes voluminous masses, motets, secular songs and instrumental music. Here is the opening of his canon for four instruments *A l'heure que je vous p.x.* (1503):

Ex 42

(Canon at the 9th with the top part)

Before 1486 he visited the ducal courts of Florence, Milan and Ferrara. In 1486 he entered the Sistine Chapel at Rome and stayed there, apart from a few interruptions, till 1494. In taking the Netherlands music to Italy, he prepared the way for the art of Palestrina. His liturgical music even begins to look and sound like a premonition of Palestrina's, as in this quotation from a Passion Motet of Josquin (1503) for male voices:

Ex 43 Do - mi - ne Je - su Chri - ste,

Adrian Willaert (c. 1480–1562), born at Bruges, was possibly a pupil of Josquin and, as he worked and died in Venice, he was another link in the Flemish influence on Italian music.

The age of Josquin saw the advent of printing. Paper manufacture made this possible. The Chinese had made paper for centuries. The Arabs learned the process from them in their

C

8th century occupation of Samarkand and brought it to Europe through the 12th century Moorish invasion of Spain. A 13th century tract of Peter, Abbot of Cluny, first mentions ragpaper. Great bundles of paper were imported and exported by the medieval world mart of Bruges, and it was in Haarlem that Coster printed from moveable type, sometime before 1446. Gutenberg was printing at Mainz about the same time. Caxton's Westminster press was set up in 1477. The Bavarian Ulrich Hahn (b. early 15th century – d. 1478) was the first music printer: he printed a missal (black square notes on red lines) at Rome in 1476. Some of Josquin's music was printed at Venice in 1503 from metal type by Ottaviano dei Petrucci. Printing fermented intellectual enquiry.

Meanwhile, in the Netherlands bell-making was perfected and the art of carillon-playing was beginning to resound. The carillon is a chromatic set of bells hung or fixed in a tower, 3 – 4 octaves in compass, and played from a keyboard and pedals (like an organ) or automatically by clockwork. Dunkerque had a carillon in 1437, Alost in 1487, Antwerp in 1540 and Bruges in 1675. These carillons played mainly Netherlands folk-music, and, sounding every hour over the town, they were the poor man's music books.

POSTSCRIPT TO FLEMISH MUSIC. The Big Four syndrome seems to operate in the arts as in politics: most people's knowledge of music (apart from popular music) is restricted to Austrian, French, German and Italian compositions. Music of the numerically smaller nations (Flemish music, for instance) or music of the historically under-privileged majorities (the Slavs, for example) is relatively unknown. The Bulgarian leader Georgi Dimitrov (1882–1949) put it well when he said: 'In culture there are, in ability, no small and great nations, no superior and inferior peoples. Every people, no matter how small, can make their contribution.'

An example of a minority whose cultural achievements are inadequately appreciated is the Walloon people, who, with Liége as their capital, were at the centre of Flemish-Belgian musical life. The roll-call of Liége musicians includes Grétry (18th century), Franck and Lekeu (19th century), and Yasye and Jongen (20th century). Ysaye, the father of modern violin-playing, composed the first opera (1931) to a Walloon libretto, *Pière li Houyeu* ('Peter the Miner'), whose plot concerns a miners' strike.

8 Palestrina and his Contemporaries

If you see Rome from an aeroplane, you get a good view of Saint Peter's and its Piazza. It's the best way of seeing the anthropomorphous aspect of the Cathedral. The dome is the head; from it, the colonnade inscribes its semicircle on each side, like embracing arms.

Fifteenth and sixteenth century Italian architects – such men as Alberti, Bramante, Brunelleschi, Michelangelo and Palladio – were all Pythagoreans in that the rationale of their theory of architecture was that proportions rule everything. This principle was also found in a ratio between architecture and music: the musical consonance of the Pythagorean intervals was the criterion for architectural consonance.

If your plane touches down at Pisa and you visit the 'leaning tower' and the Cathedral and then go into the Baptistry, the guide will sing a note, and the triform Baptistry, built like a tiara, will give back not only the echo but also the third and fifth above the echo. Here you have a concrete example of the saying ascribed to Goethe, that 'architecture is frozen music'.

When the German acoustician Helmholtz (1821–94) looked through the scores of Palestrina, he found that this 16th century music adhered to the rule that notes sound well together when the ratio of their frequencies is expressed by the simple integers, 1, 2, 3, 4. The smaller the numbers, the more consonant the sound. The octave ratio is 2:1; the fifth, 3:2. As the Soviet acoustician, Anfilov, has remarked, 'Palestrina wrote his music as if he could have seen Helmholtz's charts and tables of overtones'.

These simple ratios were not only basic to Palestrina's harmony, but also to his melody and rhythm. His melody also consisted of simple intervals and his rhythm moved within the framework of four minims to a bar or three semibreves to a bar, which were actually expressed in old manuscripts by the ratios 4:2 and 3:1. The triple metre was faster than the quadruple. The proportion was one bar of 4/2 time equals two bars of 3/1 time.

So proportion ruled Palestrina's music, just as it ruled the architecture of the Italian churches in which it was sung.

One of the features distinguishing Flemish music from Palestrina's was that the Flemish near-obsession with canon resulted in sequential writing (repetitious sound-patterns) which produced *symmetry*, whereas Palestrina's style was one of freely flowing long lines, not concatenations of little patterns, and these long lines produced *proportion*. Ruskin in *Stones of Venice* gives a clear explanation of the difference between symmetry and proportion: 'Wherever Proportion exists at all, one member of the composition must be either larger than, or in some way supreme over, the rest. There is no proportion between equal things. They can have symmetry only, and symmetry without proportion is not composition.' This must not be taken to imply that Flemish music lacked proportion or that Palestrina's music lacked symmetry. The Flemings indeed had a theory of rhythmic proportion named *prolatio*, but it operated between the relationship between *notes* in one bar, whereas Palestrina's proportion operated between *phrases* extending over two or more bars.

Palestrina was a child of the Counter Reformation. Luther burned the Papal bull at Wittenberg on 10 December 1520. Ignatius Loyola founded the order of Jesuits in 1539 to counteract Lutheranism. Palestrina was born between those two dates, in 1525 or 26 at the small cathedral town of Palestrina, situated at the foot of the Sabine mountains in the Roman Campagna. The order and control of his music runs parallel to the scholasticism engendered by the Order of Jesuits which gave a new impetus to Catholic studies. Their schools became the best in Europe by reason of their intellectual discipline. Lord Verulam (Sir Francis Bacon) wrote of these schools: 'As for the pedagogic part ... consult the schools of the Jesuits, for nothing better has been put into practice'. Members of The Society of Jesus were bound by three personal vows of poverty, chastity and obedience. The music of the Palestrinan school is as if it were written from the same vows, musically interpreted; for its technical means are modest, it has the chastity of the ecclesiastic modes instead of the sensuousness of indulged chromaticism, and it is obedient to certain musical laws. It also evinces singleness of purpose, for Palestrina wrote ecclesiastic music almost exclusively. Loyola's most celebrated work was the *Book of Spiritual Exercises*, intended for the use of initiates. This is divided into four meditations. Similarly, the musicologists of Palestrina's time – such men as Zacconi and Zarlino – codified what might be termed a 'book of polyphonic exercises', likewise intended for students; and this was also divided into sections, which became known as the 'five species' of counterpoint. These five species demonstrate different counterpoints to a tenor *cantus fermus*, each of the five species becoming progressively more complex than its predecessor. First species presents note against note (itself a definition of counterpoint or point-counter-point). Second species presents two notes against one. Third species four notes against one. Fourth species, two notes against one but with syncopations or ligatures (every other note of the counterpoint is tied over or sustained into the successive note). Fifth species is a synthesis of the first four. Here follow examples by Palestrina's contemporary, Ludovico Zacconi (1555–1627), from his book *Prattica di musica* (Venice, 1592).

Ex 44.

I First species

II Second species

After having mastered the two-part technique in fifth species, the student would then proceed to the five species in three parts. This method is perhaps the only really teachable technique of composition and is still used in music education four centuries afterwards. Here is an example of Palestrina's three part polyphonic style, from the Benedictus in his Missa 'Lauda Sion':

The cases of percussed dissonnance (indicated by the asterisk) are exceptions to Palestrina's generally unpercussed style.

Though it is permissible to generalize about Palestrina's style — and there are innumerable textbooks on the subject — there are more than one Palestrina style, though they operate within a narrow range. Tradition has it that he was a chorister at the church of Santa Maria Maggiore in Rome. Research indicates that he studied composition with a Flemish master in Rome between 1540 and 1544; possibly with Gaudio Mel or Arcadelt. Flemish features are traceable in his early works such as the Missa brevis (1554), in which the *amen* of the *Credo* contains typically Flemish canonic sequence.

Palestrina's employment in the Church of Rome was riddled with vicissitude, largely due to his being a married man at a time when ecclesiastic strictures favoured celibates, not only in the priesthood but also in other offices. Palestrina married in 1547. In 1551 Pope Julius III elected him choir master at the Capella Giulia, San Pietro in Vaticano. A house went with the job: the salary was modest. His *First Book of Masses* (1554) is dedicated to Julius, who, in 1555, elected him to the post of Singer in the Sistine Chapel. His previous post was filled by his friend Animuccia. The new appointment was legally disputed because of the celibacy preference. Pope Julius was succeeded by Marcellus II and by Paul IV, who dismissed Palestrina in 1555, together with other married singers, though a small consolatory pension was granted. Palestrina had four children by this time. Unemployed, he became ill. But later in the same year he was appointed choir master to the Lateran and, in February 1561, to Santa Maria Maggiore. He remained there for 10 years and wrote his greatest work there.

In 1562 the Council of Trent censured the prevalent style of church music. In 1564 Pius IV instituted a commission to investigate the complaint. It was proposed to ban all music except unaccompanied plainsong. Some of the commission members invited Palestrina to submit the kind of music he thought suitable. He submitted his greatest work, the *Missa Papa Marcelli* (1562), which Pius IV compared to the music St. John heard in his vision of the New Jerusalem. Palestrina's polyphonic style had attained fulfilment.

Animuccia died in 1571 and Palestrina was re-elected to his appointment at the Capella Giulia and also succeeded Animuccia as choirmaster of the Oratory of Filippa Neri. 1580 was a bad year: Palestrina's wife and three of his sons died; he was left with one son. He re-married in 1581. In 1586 the possibility of his being appointed conductor of the pontifical choir was frustrated by intrigue among the musicians. He died in 1594.

His later music is more homophonic than polyphonic, i.e. music in block chords in which harmony predominates over counterpoint. In this he differs from most composers, who generally become more polyphonic towards the end of their life. His *Stabat Mater* is a notable example of his homophonic style. Tovey described this work as 'one of the simplest compositions in the world, the purest cloudscape in the world of harmony, without even a flight of birds to show the scale of its mighty perspective'.

Palestrina also wrote madrigals in this homophonic style, some secular, some spiritual, as in his settings of Petrarch's *Sonnets to the Virgin*. The madrigal developed originally about 1530, from the fusion of motet and such light song-forms as the Italian *villanella* or *frottola* or the French *chanson*.

If reading the exegesis of Palestrina's music in this chapter has created the impression that it is a thing of rules and calculations, another quotation from Tovey should be borne in mind: 'To me Palestrina was a mere mass of grammatical propositions until I heard a choir in the apse of a cathedral.'

Palestrina's greatest contemporary was the Belgian Orlando Lasso, or di Lasso or Lassus (c. 1530–1594). Unlike Palestrina, he travelled much and was extremely versatile in the types of music he wrote. Born in Mons, he was appointed to the Church of St. John Lateran in Rome as a young man, visited England, had his first madrigals published in Venice in 1555, his first motets published in Antwerp in 1556, settled at the Ducal Court of Munich probably in 1557, but still paid long visits to Italy and France. He married in 1558 and had six children. His four sons became musicians and the two eldest published their father's large collection of motets, the *Magnum opus musicum*. At Munich he had every facility for music-making. His earlier music is secular, his later sacred. He gradually achieved a purity of polyphonic style approaching Palestrina, though his natural proclivity was to secular composition. The French poet Ronsard was a friend and he set some of his *chansons*. His range encompasses the burlesque and the sublime. His burlesque motet *S.U. Su. P.E.R. per super F.L.U.* is a parody of stammering, one verse taking fifteen minutes! His *Penitential Psalms* are examples of his writing at its most sublime.

The Spaniard Tommasso Ludovico da Victoria (c. 1540–1611) was the most distinguished of a host of composers influenced by Palestrina. He held appointments at the Collegium Germanicum, Rome, and the Royal Chapel, Madrid. His Requiem for the Empress Maria (1603) is probably his greatest work. He confined himself to ecclesiastic music.

Meanwhile, the Netherlands school, while having been absorbed into Italian music, was by no means extinct on its own territory. Claude Le Jeune (1528–1602) was born at Valenciennes which was then Flanders, not France. During the wars of the Catholic League in the 1580's his sympathies were pro-Huguenot. In the siege of Paris (1588) he was arrested by Catholic soldiers and his MSS would have been confiscated if his Catholic colleague, Jacques Mandit, had not intervened. His metrical Psalms were published at La Rochelle, the seat of French Protestantism. His sister Cecile edited his published music. His 39 chansons are notable for their irregular rhythms, as in this quotation from his *O rôze, reyne des fleurs* (1603):

Ex 46

O rô ze rey ne des fleurs

In the 16th century, Venice was a centre of world trade. The grandiose Adriatic republic, ruled by the Doge, was on good terms with the Turks, who put pressure on Europe after they had brought about the fall of Constantinople in 1453. The splendour of 16th century Venice found its musical expression in the music of the Gabrieli family: Andrea (c. 1510–1586) a pupil of Willaert; and Andrea's nephew, Giovanni (1557–1612). The Gabrielis wrote for antiphonal (answering or echoing) choirs of voices and instruments, mainly brass. These sonorities were conceived in terms of the Byzantine/Romanesque architecture of St. Mark's Cathedral, with its nave divided into three square bays, with additional bays on north and south, forming transepts. These spacious bays were covered with oriental-looking domes, with wide transverse barrel vaults, covered with lead. The work of Gabrieli the Younger owed no allegiance to the austere Palestrinan beauty of sound of the High Renaissance but boldly created a Baroque style in Italian music.

Another example of this new Baroque style was Carlo Gesualdo, Prince of Venosa, (c. 1560–1614), a colourful character who was both musician and murderer. The individual chromatic harmonies of his madrigals were in part suggested by his prowess as a lute-player, chromatic sliding from fret to fret being easy on the lute. A typical example is the close of his madrigal *Dolcissima mia vita* (Venice, 1611):

9 The Tudor School and their Continental Contemporaries

Raleigh's mantle thrown on the mud, as a regal carpet, is a symbol of the whole Elizabethan epoch, which covered squalor with splendour. The stench of London rose from insanitation and from the tributaries of the Thames being choked with refuse. Some of the covered sewers of to-day were open sewers at that time. The *pickadil*, a stiff, pointed, Spanish collar, was already being sported in the fashionable promenade of Piccadilly, to which it gave its name. It was an age of animal appetites. Humour was coarse. Both ale and blood flowed in taverns. The Elizabethan era witnessed a sudden burst of energy. Basic to it all was the establishment of England as the world's leading maritime power under Drake and Frobisher. In 1563, Drake and Hawkins imported potatoes from Santa Fé, New Mexico; in 1583 Raleigh imported tobacco grown by the Red Indians of Virginia ('tobacco' is a Red Indian name), and a new fragrance filled the air of London. Music, too, was imported. A Sussex man, Nicholas Yonge (Young), living in the Cornhill district of London, imported printed books of Italian madrigals, which he translated and published in two volumes in 1588 and 1597, as *Musica Transalpina*. The lute hung on the walls of barbers' shops, to be taken down and played by the customer awaiting attention. Elizabeth herself played the virginals and was said to be jealous of the virginals-playing of Mary Queen of Scots. Perhaps Elizabeth inherited something from her father, Henry VIII, who was a composer of music for voices and viols. Henry VI was also a composer and Henry V (of the House of Lancaster) maintained a full musical establishment in his Chapter Royal.

The Tudor period began with the Reign of Henry VII in 1485 and ended with Elizabeth's death in 1603; but the leading composers in the Tudor school lived on into the reign of James I of England and VI of Scotland.

There are three main categories in the Tudor school: the madrigalists, the virginalists and the lutenists. (The virginals was the smallest harpsichord with a plectra-mechanism for plucking the strings.)

William Byrd (1542–1623) was the most considerable Tudor polyphonist. He was also the most versatile and industrious of the school, his work including examples of all the forms of the period. He wrote madrigals, masses, motets, lute songs, preludes, dances, fantasies and variations for virginals. The English chronicler Anthony à Wood, avers that Byrd was 'bred up to musick under Thomas Tallis'. Both Byrd and Tallis (c. 1505–1585) were organists, Byrd at Lincoln Cathedral, Tallis at Waltham Abbey. In the 1570's they were joint organists at the Chapel Royal and also business associates, for they were granted a licence for printing music and music paper in England. In 1575 they jointly published a set of motets, 16 by Tallis, 18 by Byrd. When Tallis died, Byrd inherited sole rights of the printing business but assigned them to Thomas East in 1588. In the same year Byrd contributed two madrigals to Yonge's *Musica Transalpina*. Being a Catholic, Byrd's position in the Chapel Royal was precarious. His house was searched on a number of occasions and his career was also frustrated with law suits respecting property. He remained secure probably only through the protection of influential friends, such as the Earl of Northampton and the Earl of Cumberland, both dedicatees of his work. His will provided well for his wife and five children.

The syntax of Byrd's choral polyphony is not as strict, not so systematic, as Palestrina's. There are more percussed dissonances in Byrd than in Palestrina, freer treatment of the vocally difficult tritone interval (F-B or F sharp – C), free use of major/minor relationships and a characteristic recurrence of pentatonically inclined melodic fragments, as at the places marked by asterisk in the following quotation from his Motet, *Alleluia quae lucescit*:

Ex 48

Byrd's great range of style may be demonstrated by comparing the austerity of the last example with his variations for virginals on the popular London street song, *The Carman's Whistle*.

Thomas Morley (1557–1603) was a pupil of Byrd, and, like most of the leading Tudor composers, a gentleman of the Chapel Royal. He was also probably organist at St. Paul's. His pedagogic gift was remarkable, as may be seen from his *Plaine and Easie Introduction to Musicke* (1597). He was one of the leading madrigalists and his madrigals, canzonets and ballets show how, with the adaptation of the Italian madrigal to the English language, its rhythms became freer, especially in the interpenetrating cross-rhythms of the part-writing. The *phrase*, not the bar-line, decides accentuation. Morley also wrote some songs for Shakespeare plays and music for viol consort (a family of viols of different sizes).

Social content in the poetic texts of the Tudor madrigals often gives a false picture. The shepherd's life, in particular, is represented in the idyllic mood of the Spenserian pastoral at a time when 'the work of a whole year would not supply the agricultural labourer with what he could have earned a hundred years earlier with fifteen weeks' labour' (Thorold Rogers: *Six Centuries of Work and Wages*). No Tudor musician matched Shakespeare in his understanding of the common man.

Consort music was cultivated extensively by the leisured classes with families of recorders and viols. Sometimes the consorts were complete; sometimes the instrumental groups were mixed, with an ensemble formed from incomplete (or 'broken') consorts.

This was an age, not only of families of instruments, but of families of musicians, also. Two of the most famous Tudor musical families were the Ferraboscos (from Italy) and the Gibbonses.

'Master' Alfonso Ferrabosco (as he was known) was a friend of Byrd. He travelled back and forth from Italy and died in Turin in 1588. He is basic to the 'transalpine' influx of Italian influence on the English madrigal. His sons Alfonso and Henry were known to the diarist Pepys. Alfonso the Younger's son John was organist of Ely Cathedral.

Another musical family of this age was that of the Spanish de Cabezóns. Antonio de Cabezón (1510–1566) was a blind organist who, after studying with Tomas Gomez, became organist and clavichordist to Charles V and Philipp II, whom he accompanied to England in 1554–5. Tallis would presumably have heard him. Cabezón developed contrapuntal writing for keyboard instruments. His younger brother Juan and son Hernando were also composers.

The Gibbons family emanated from Cambridge. The most celebrated member of it was Orlando Gibbons (1583–1625). At 12 he was a chorister at King's College, Cambridge. At 21 he was appointed organist of the Chapel Royal. In 1622 Gibbons received an honorary doctorate in music at Oxford, through his friend Camden, founder of the Chair of History at that University. Heyther, founder and first incumbent of the Oxford Chair of Music also received a doctorate on this occasion, and, as Heyther was musically unskilled, Gibbon's eight-part anthem *O clap your hands* was permitted to serve as Heyther's 'commencement' song. Such were the machinations of seats of learning. Gibbon's last public appearance was as conductor on the occasion of the funeral of James I in 1625. His madrigals, motets and virginals music is harmonically expressive and rhythmically flexible constituting an outstanding contribution to the music of the Tudor school.

John Bull – the name which in Napoleonic times became synonymous with British jingoism – was the leading Elizabethan instrumental composer. He was born c. 1562, perhaps in Somerset, travelled much and died in 1628 in Antwerp. He was educated in Queen Elizabeth's Chapel. In 1582 he was organist of Hereford Cathedral, in 1585 a member of the Chapel Royal, where he became organist in 1591. In 1586 he graduated as bachelor of music and in 1592 as doctor of music at Oxford. He was the first professor of music at Gresham College, for which post his lack of normally required Latin was conveniently overlooked. He travelled to France and Germany and was a living legend because of his keyboard virtuosity. He has been called the 'Franz Liszt' of his day. He returned to England, and wrote anthems for royal occasions. About 1614 he left England rather mysteriously, perhaps after a royal row, and never returned. Mystery surrounds his private life. He became organist to the Archduke's Chapel at Brussels and in 1617 was appointed organist at Antwerp Cathedral. His jig, *The King's Hunt*, contains in embryo much that later keyboard music developed: scales, arpeggi, double 3rds and 6ths, repeated notes and ingenious passage work. The 'programme' – element in the piece is also evocative, as in this suggestion of the barking of the hounds:

Bull and the Dutch organist Jan Pieterzoon Sweelinck (1562–1621) became intimates and there may have been some mutual influence between them. Sweelinck was an innovator in his employment of an independent pedal part in organ music. He also contributed to the development of fugue form, as in his *Fantasia cromatica*:

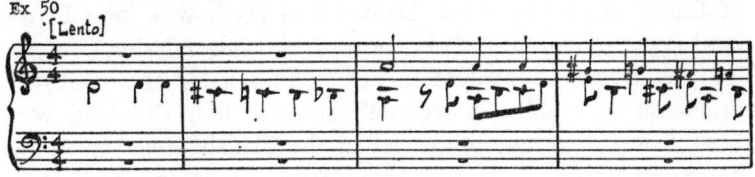

A piece of Sweelinck's is included in the famous Fitzwilliam Virginal Book, a manuscript housed in the Fitzwilliam Museum, Cambridge. This, formerly 'Queen Elizabeth's Virginal Book', is one of the two main sources of original virginals music. It is written on 6-line staves, bound in crimson morocco tooled in gold fleur-de-lis.

The other source of virginals music is *Parthenia*, the first collection of it that was printed from plates engraved by William Hole. It appeared in 1611 – the same year as the King James Bible – and was reprinted five times between then and 1689.

The most frequent dance forms of the virginalists were the Pavan and Galliard. The origin of the Spanish Pavan, which generally had four beats to the bar, was probably the Latin word *pavo*, meaning 'peacock', with reference to the resemblance to the peacock's fanned tail made by the dresses of the dancers as they moved in the stately measure.

The Galliard was originally the Roman *gagliarda*-dance. The word implies a bold, vigorous, merry measure. It was generally in 3 beats to the bar but sometimes in 2 or 4. It followed, and contrasted with, the Pavan, as the Gigue later followed the Saraband in the Baroque suite.

Giles Farnaby (c. 1560–1640) is another of the leading virginalists and madrigalists. His keyboard pieces often have fanciful poetic titles, like those later used by Couperin and, much later, by Debussy.

The most outstanding lutenist among the celebrated names of Campian and Rosseter, Danyel and Ford, was John Dowland (1562–1626). The dedication of his song *Pilgrimes Solace* 'to my loving countreyman, Mr. John Forster the younger, merchant of Dublin in Ireland' indicates that Dowland was Irish. His autograph, preserved in the British Museum, spells his name 'Doland'. He was lute-player, singer and composer.

As a youth he was employed by two English Ambassadors in Paris, Sir Henry Cobham and Sir Edward Stafford. He became a convert to Catholicism. Sometime in the 1580's he returned to England and married. But he was not appreciated in England; Henry Peacham, in *Minerva Britanna* (1612), compares him to a nightingale on a briar in winter. This neglect was probably the reason why Dowland travelled a great deal. He performed for the Duke of Brunswick who rewarded him with a gold chain, £23, velvet, satin and gold lace; performed for the Landgrave of Hessen, who presented him with a gold cup full of money and sent Mrs. Dowland a fine ring; and performed for the Duke of Florence, where Dowland 'got great favours'. His travels took him to Bologna, Venice and Nuremberg. From 1598 to 1612 he was lutenist at the court of Christian IV, King of Denmark. English recognition of Dowland only came to him in 1612, when he was 50, with his appointment to the King's Musicians for the Lutes. His son Robert succeeded him in this post. John Dowland published three *Books of Songs Or Ayres* (1597, 1600, 1603) and further songs in *A Musical Banquet* (1610), a total of 87 songs. He also wrote some lute music. Many of his songs were written in two versions: one for solo voice and lute; the other for four voices in simple harmonization, with the melody in the soprano. An example of the second type is his *Now, o now I needs must part* (1597):

Some of his harmonies are daring and exploratory and a few of his songs add viols to the lute accompaniment. Lute music was printed in *tablature*, a system which shows the performer where his finger presses the string on a 'table' of sounds.

Dowland's songs are sensitive word settings and he was the first composer to write expressive accompaniments, which sometimes even assumed equal importance to the vocal line, as in his song *Can she excuse me wrongs?* where for a few bars the voice sings one note, while the lute comments with a quotation from the folk-song *Shall I go walk the woods so wild?*

Unlike composers of the generation previous to his, such as Byrd, who prized polyphony above melody, and unlike some of his contemporaries, such as Bull, who developed keyboard technique, Dowland turned his gift to the song form. When one remembers how Ireland has enriched the heritage of song with a more voluminous legacy of folk tunes than any other English speaking country, and, when one remembers such later collections as Moore's *Irish Melodies* and such mastery of both *bel canto* and the common touch as were John MacCormack's, it seems right that the Irishman Dowland should be the first of a line of great song composers. Schubert and Gershwin were of Dowland's lineage; and very few others.

10 The beginnings of Opera and Ballet

We begin this chapter with a bit of science. One day in 1581 Galileo Galilei sat in the Cathedral at Pisa, watching a lamp swinging. He observed that the lamp's different oscillations took the same time – an observation that led to his founding the science of dynamics.

Now about the same time that Galileo was conducting his first experiments, his father, Vincenzo Galilei, who was a musician, was holding regular meetings in the palace of Count Bardi of Vernio in Florence, with a group of composers. Among them were Jacopo Peri (1561–1633) and Giulio Caccini (c. 1558–c. 1615). They discussed the possibility of re-creating the Greek drama with its musical accompaniment of the chanting chorus. From these discussions, opera was born.

With the poet Rinuccini, Peri composed the first opera, *Dafne*. This was privately performed in the Palazzo Corsi in 1597. Unfortunately, the score is lost. Encouraged by the reception of this work, Peri and Caccini joined Rinuccini to write another opera, *Euridice*, which was performed in Florence in 1600 as part of the wedding festivities of Henry IV of France and Maria de' Medici. This score is extant. The prologue to *Euridice* opens:

So we can make the categorical statement: opera was born in Florence in 1600.

Its antecedents were: the medieval mystery plays or moralities; the pastoral, a play with incidental music, performed in princely garden-theatres; and the madrigal.

Caccini, Peri's collaborator was a madrigalist rather than an opera composer. His collection *Le nuove musiche* ('New music'), published in 1601, helped to establish the supremacy of 17th century monody over polyphony. His most famous solo madrigal *Amarilli* was published in 1602:

This kind of writing, often highly ornamented by the singer, was a development of the Dowland *ayre*.

There was much intertraffic of madrigals at the beginning of the 17th century. For example, Caccini's *Amarilli* was freely transcribed for virginals in 1603 by the English composer Peter Philips (c. 1560–c. 1635):

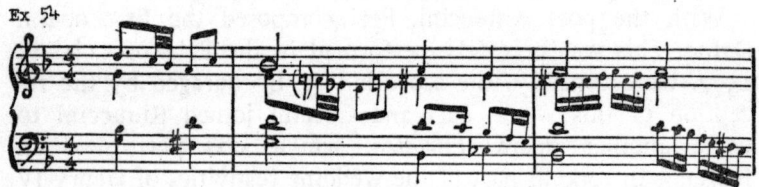

A comparison of the last two examples will reveal how free Philip's transcription is; which may come as a surprise to people who regard transcription as a form of 19th century aberration or sacrilege practised by one composer on the music of another. The truth is that this sense of property and propriety has nothing to do with music, and transcription is an art long practised by composers and, at its best, a genre of variation form. The work of a transcriber of originality

THE BEGINNINGS OF OPERA AND BALLET

can sometimes be more creative than the material on which it is based.

Claudio Monteverdi (1567-1643) began as a madrigalist but went on to develop opera. His first opera *Arianna* was composed for the wedding festivities of Francesco Gonzaga and Margherita, Infanta of Savoy, at the Court of Mantua in 1607. Here is the opening of Ariadne's Lament from this opera:

Ex 55

Monteverdi's use of unprepared dissonance, as at the places marked by asterisk in the last example, was innovatory; but it was not experiment for experiment's sake. Unprepared dissonance (a discord 'out of the blue', as it were) was necessitated by the heightened declamation Monteverdi wished to achieve in order to express the passions. It also propelled a sense of movement necessitated by opera.

In a way, the difference between the music of Palestrina and that of Monteverdi mirrors the difference between pre-Galilean and post-Galilean cosmology. Pre-Galilean cosmology was based on a static earth; post-Galilean cosmology, on a moving earth. The ecclesiastic music of Palestrina, in comparison with the operatic music of Monteverdi, is static; Monteverdi's music has a Galilean dynamism.

In performance, Monteverdi's declamatory operatic style would certainly be interpreted with a greater range of dynamics (accentuation, volume-differentiation) than was deemed appropriate for Palestrina. And in addition to his greater dynamic range, Monteverdi was an innovator in orchestral techniques. These instrumental innovations were first carried out by Monteverdi in 1624 in *Il Combattimento di Tancredi e Clorinda*, a dramatic *scena*, a kind of oratorio/opera based on a poem of Tasso. He was a violinist and was the first to indicate *pizzicato* and *tremolando* in his scores. The device of plucking the strings, creating an effect of palpitation, excitement or suspense, and the other device of rapid reiterations of bowing, creating a dramatic, rustling sound, added colour to Monteverdi's music. He was in some ways the father of the orchestra, the first to organize an orchestral ensemble; though his orchestra would sound very different from the modern symphony orchestra. The main difference would be that Monteverdi's orchestra would have a predominantly *plucked* sound, resulting from the use of lute and harpsichord as basic background sonority, whereas the symphony orchestra has a more *sustained* sound. Plucked sound provides in some ways a better background for singing than the modern orchestra does, because plucked sound contrasts better with the *sustained* sound of the voice.

In 1608 Monteverdi brought out his second opera, *Orfeo* (libretto by Striggio), also at Mantua. This was the same subject as Peri's *Euridice* but a much more dramatic treatment of it.

Vicenzo I of Mantua died in 1612. His successor relieved Monteverdi of his duties. In 1613 he was appointed *maestro di capella* at St. Mark's, Venice, where he composed much liturgical music. He maintained connection with Mantua, however, and in 1615 wrote the opera-ballet *Tirso e Clori*, commissioned by Ferdinand Gonzega. Venice acquired its opera house in 1637, the first public one (under the management of two musicians, Ferrari and da Tivoli.) Manelli's *Andromeda* was chosen for the inauguration. This event acted as a catalyst to Monteverdi's renewed efforts at operatic composition. In between work at operas, Monteverdi added to his corpus of madrigals, mainly in 5-part writing. There was a *Faustian* duality in him, which was symbolized by his being ordained priest in 1622 and yet by pursuing his composition of operas after this date. This Faustian aspect found a subject equal to it in *Il Ritorno d'Ulisse in Patria* (libretto by Badoaro), 1641. His last opera was *L'incoronazione di Poppea*, 1642.

Declamation, which first sounded in the operas of Monteverdi, has re-echoed in the operas of later Italian masters, such as Rossini, Verdi, and Puccini.

The Italian word 'opera' simply signifies 'a work'. The word 'ballet' derives via the Sicilian from the Greek. A cognate word is 'ballad', originally dance-song, later a narrative song. Just as opera is drama in song, ballet is drama in dance. The earliest ballet, if we exclude the Greek Dance, was presented by Bergonzio di Botta at Tortona, Italy, in 1489, to celebrate the marriage of the Duke of Milan.

Jean-Baptiste Lully (1639-1687) was a naturalized French composer, born in Florence and died in Paris, who developed both opera and ballet. His origins were obscure, probably poor, for he kept silent about them. An Italian cobbler-monk taught the boy the guitar. The Chevalier de Guise discovered him and took him back to France when Lully was only a boy of 12 or so. He entered the service of the Chevalier's niece as a kitchen scullion. From this employment he gradually inveigled himself into aristocratic society, until he gained the confidence of Louis XIV, who put him in charge of the court music, granted him naturalization papers and a noble title and made him his private secretary. Louis also decreed that Lully should monopolize French opera by the Royal command that no opera should be performed without Lully's permission. It is one of music's most improbable stories. It certainly argues that Lully was an astute judge of human foibles, a master hand in the game of social chess, and perhaps something of a rogue. He was also a theatrical character, both in life and in the theatre. In addition to being a composer, conductor and violinist, he was also an actor and ballet dancer. He was the resident composer in one of the greatest theatrical companies of all time – Molière's. To Molière, Lully was '*le cher Baptiste*'. In the premiere of Molière's *Le Bourgeois Gentilhomme*, Lully played and danced the part of Master of the Turkish Ceremony.

Louis XIV was not only a 'balletomane' but an enthusiastic ballerino himself. Wherever the court went, Molière and Lully followed. The productions in the garden theatre at Versailles had an opulence which may be glimpsed in the engravings of the period, preserved in the Hennin Collection at the Bibliotheque Nationale, Paris. This theatre of canvas and foliage was the work of the master architects, Le Notre and Vigarani. Cypresses were cut to match the production, as part of the *mise-en-scène*. For the allegory, *Les Plaisirs de l'Ile Enchantée*, engraved in 1664 by Israël Silvestre, there were a hundred crystal chandeliers with four thousand candles which transformed night into day. The *corps de ballet* numbered four dozen. Lully conducted an orchestra of thirty-four musicians. This spectacle was held over three days. On the third day the performance included a marine drama, with Alcine and her servants riding a realistic sea-monster.

Lully matched these scenes with music of style. He learned much from the operas of the Venetian Cavalli (1603–76), who brought Monteverdi's influence to France. The following quotation from the final section of the Lament of Merope from Lully's opera *Persée* (Paris, 1682) demonstrates what he had absorbed of Monteverdi's declamatory style:

Lully lacked Monteverdi's intensity but his specific contribution to opera was the rhythmic variety which resulted from his experience as a dancer and actor. The most significant aspect of Lully's career was that he was the first composer who was a man of the theatre. The theatre is so complex a medium that the most convincing work in it has always been done by people who have had theatre in their blood. With the court poet Quinault, Lully wrote more than twenty operas. He developed accompanied recitative (a speech-like, stylized narrative in song, as distinct from an aria or melody), whereas his Italian predecessors had preferred unaccompanied recitative. He established the French overture form, with its characteristically majestic and heroic introduction in alternating slow and quick notes, contrasted with a following fugal *allegro*. The French overture evolved into the *sonata da chiesa*, or church sonata, for one or more violins and bass, in three movements: a French overture, a slow song-like movement and a quick finale. Lully also wrote some liturgical music. The ballet suite, which he esablished, evolved into the *sonata da camera*, or chamber sonata, which was a string of dance movements.

With Bach and Handel, both the French overture and the suite reached full fruition half a century later. Examples of the French overture are the orchestral introduction to Handel's *Messiah* and the imposing variation that opens the second half of Bach's 'Goldberg' Variations for harpsichord. The keyboard suites of Bach and Handel are also of the lineage of Lully.

Ballet, which Lully first introduced into opera as a divertissement, has played a traditional role in French opera down to Berlioz's *Les Troyens* and Gounod's *Faust*, in the 19th century.

After Lully, the next development of opera took place in England, in the work of Henry Purcell (1658–95). He came of a musical family. He lived in turbulent times. In Purcell's birth-year, Cromwell died. In 1666 there was the Great Fire of London. Purcell's father was a gentleman of the Chapel Royal, who died when the son was a young lad; so Purcell was reared by his uncle, who was also a gentleman of the Chapel Royal. Purcell was a boy chorister there. He was a pupil of Pelham Humphrey who in turn had been a pupil of Lully. Purcell also studied under Dr. John Blow. In 1676 he was appointed copyist at Westminster Abbey. In the same year he began to collaborate with John Dryden, Poet Laureate, on theatre works, such as *Aureng-zebe*, *The Indian Queen*, *Tyrannic Love*, *King Arthur*, and for Dryden's adaptations from Shakespeare, such as *The Fairy Queen* (from *The Midsummer Night's Dream*) and a version of *The Tempest*. In 1682 Purcell was appointed organist of the Chapel Royal. In this capacity, he wrote many anthems, some for his friend, the Rev. Gostling, a *basso profondo* of extraordinary range. The most outstanding of these anthems is *They that go down to the sea in ships*, which exploits the bass voice from the D above the bass stave down two octaves to the D below the bass stave. Purcell also wrote some almost fragrant harpsichord suites, chamber music, sonatas and fantazias for strings which extend the lineage of the older school of music for viol consorts. These fantazias are pure string music, written at a time when orchestral music did not dominate instrumental music to the extent that music for solo instruments embodied attempts to imitate the orchestra. Examples of this kind of imitation may be found in the violinistic phrasing of Bach's keyboard works, the 'horn-call'-like phrases in Beethoven's piano sonatas, the symphonically orchestral piano style of Liszt and the string quartet of Greig which in its double-stoppings, – i.e. a string instrument played on two or more strings simultaneously – emulates the sonorities of a string orchestra. It may be said that this kind of composition, in which an instrument imitates another instrument, or ensemble, is thereby an enriched form of writing. That may be so. But there should be room in the world of music for different styles and manners. Purcell's string writing is pure string style in the same way that Chopin's piano writing is purely pianistic. That is, it is a thing in terms of itself, not in terms of something else. And it is as refreshing to meet music that is itself as it is to meet a person who is himself.

Purcell, unlike the later Bach or Beethoven, did not write 'instrumentally' for the voice. His string music is just that; it is free from extraneous 'effects', so is his vocal music. He developed considerably the musical setting of the English language and, in this, brought to fulfilment the work of such predecessors as John Merbecke and Henry Lawes and, in turn, laid the ground for its further development in Handel and in a much later composer, Benjamin Britten. According to contemporary evidence in *The Gentleman's Journal and Monthly Miscellany* of November 1692. Purcell was himself an accomplished singer and sang 'with incredible graces' (ornamentation of the melody). Many of his rounds and 'catches' (another name for round) must have been composed for his own circle of friends.

His outstanding opera is *Dido and Aeneas* (1680). The libretto is based on a play by Nahum Tate. This opera was written for a Chelsea girls' boarding school, run by a Mr. Josias Priest. Such a parochial setting for one of the world's great operas is peculiarly English and reflects on the structure of a state which has never nurtured opera as it has been nurtured in Italy or Germany and other countries. We find the same situation in the 20th century, with Rutland Boughton producing his operas in the village hall of Glastonbury and with Benjamin Britten producing operas in the local halls and churches of Aldeburgh. Though one would welcome tangible state encouragement of British opera, one must admit that something peculiarly English has resulted from operas that have been staged under these restricting parochial conditions. It has produced an intimate kind of opera which reflects the rather shy psychology of the English. The quintessence of this shy spirit is found in Dido's Lament from Purcell's opera, which, incidentally, is built on a ground bass (one of Purcell's favoured devices, a reiterated bass line, which remains constant, and over which the melody moves freely):

Ex 57

Gordon Craig's legendary production of *Dido and Aeneas* in London in 1900 was, according to contemporary accounts, one of the peaks of modern operatic production. W. B. Yeats wrote of 'Gordon Craig's purple backcloth that made Dido and Aeneas seem wandering on the edge of eternity'.

11 The Baroque and Rococo styles

The Baroque style flourished in Italian, then in German music in the 17th and early 18th centuries. The Rococo style flourished in France, then in Germany in the 18th century. The two terms are sometimes treated as synonymous, but there is some reason to regard the Rococo as a prettification of the Baroque. The word 'baroque' derives from the Spanish *barrueco*, a large, irregularly shaped pearl. The word 'rococo' derives from the French *rocaille*, a rockery. 'Baroque' originally implied pearl culture and therefore an organic growth; 'rococo', a man-made, stylized rockery. The same distinction can also be read into baroque and rococo music: what seems like ornamentation in baroque music is often an organic part of its structure, but the ornamentation of rococo music is more purely decorative. Both are highly ornamental, but the Baroque is grandly flamboyant, where the Rococo is elegantly decorative.

Baroque music is like a giant pearl washed ashore from a great rack. That great rack was the Thirty Years' War which laid Germany waste from its formal inception with the claim of Frederick the Elector Palatine to the throne of Bavaria in 1618, to its cessation with the Treaty of Westphalia in 1648. It was a civil war of religion and politics, akin to the civil war in England (1642–49) and to the war of the Fronde (1648–55) in France. All these wars pitted a Protestant nobility against a Catholic crown. In England and Holland Protestantism succeeded, in France Catholicism, but in Germany nobody won. Everybody lost. The emperor lacked power, the nobility lacked unity. Unpaid soldiers plundered. The land was neglec-

THE BAROQUE AND ROCOCO STYLES 93

ted or abandoned. What meagre crops were grown were hidden. The German landscape was populated by human scarecrows, starving women and children.

It is a testimony to the fortitude of humanity that, in the wake of such desolation, some of the most glorious music began to resound in Germany. This phoenix-period in German music found its spiritual impulse in rising from the ashes of the Thirty Years' War, but the *technical* basis came from Italy. This was an era of intertraffic between Italian and German composers.

As Albert Schweitzer writes in his book on Bach, 'in the person of Heinrich Schütz (1585 – 1673), German art itself crossed the Alps'. This was in 1609, at the behest of the Landgrave Moritz of Hesse-Cassel. Schütz studied in Venice with Giovanni Gabrieli and Monteverdi. Gabrieli bequeathed baroque poly phony to German music through Schütz, Monteverdi bequeathed the dramatic instinct. From Gabriel's influence Schütz developed the spiritual madrigal; from Monteverdi's influence he laid the foundation of German opera, composing the first work in the genre, *Daphne*. This opera was produced in Torgau in 1627. Its score is now lost. The text by Opitz, based on the Italian of Rinuccini, is all that remains. In the ravages of the Thirty Years' War, engraving of music was scarce and many manuscripts were lost or destroyed. Fortunately, through Schütz's many wanderings and appointments to different courts – even as far away as Copenhagen – some of his MSS have been preserved: the *Seven Last Words* in Cassel and other works in Wölfenbüttel. He set texts from Luther's Bible as it stood, principally the Davidic Psalms and the Gospels. The fashion for biblical paraphrases came later. He did not interest himself in the chorale, as did his contemporary Michael Praetorius. whose chorale-carol *Es ist ein Ros' entsprungen* remains a favourite German Christmas song. For the Schlosskirche at Dresden, Schütz composed church concertos, precursors of the German cantata.

Meanwhile, in Italy, both instrumental music and opera were being developed with fresh impetus. Claudio Merulo (1533–1604) and Girolamo Frescobaldi (1583–1644) developed organ music in Rome. Frescobaldi in particular wrote many brilliant *toccatas* (from *toccare*, to touch the keyboard; meaning a virtuosic piece to display the performer's prowess).

Arcangelo Corelli (1653–1713) virtuoso violinist/composer, travelled much as a young man, was attached to the court of the Elector of Bavaria at Munich, visited Paris and left it summarily when Lully turned jealous, and settled in Rome, where many musicians met him, including Handel. Corelli was the father of the violin, though his technique was limited. His writing for violin never exploits the highest notes. He founded the concerto grosso form, which contrasted a small group of performers (the *concertino* or small concerted group of two or three players) with the *concerto* or *ripieno* (the large or full concerted group of players). The Venetian, Antonio Vivaldi (c. 1678–1743) was a more showy performer than Corelli and extended the solo passages in the concerto grosso until the solo violin dominated. Handel and Bach developed the concerto grosso, Bach making many transcriptions for keyboard and orchestra of Vivaldi's violin concertos.

After Monteverdi's death, the next step in the progress of Italian opera was made by Alessandro Scarlatti (1659–1725). His main contribution was the establishment of the *da capo* aria (the solo operatic song which repeated its opening section at the end). The operas of Scarlatti exercised a major influence on Mozart, half-a-century later.

Alessandro Scarlatti's son, Domenico (1685–1757) is the third great composer born in 1685; the other two being Bach and Handel. One often reads of Bach and Handel as 'the heavenly twins', Scarlatti being overlooked. His originality went largely unsuspected – despite Longo's devoted (if not always faithful) editorship early in the present century – until the American scholar/harpsichordist, Ralph Kirkpatrick, brought out his biography and edition of the Scarlatti Sonatas. During the first half of his life, Domenico Scarlatti was a pale imitation of his illustrious father; like him, writing operas and church music. During the last half of his life he found himself by living in Spain and writing harpsichord music. He wrote over 500 harpsichord Sonatas, all of them miniatures. Centuries before the camera, they exhibit the musical equivalent of the photographer's art of capturing the fleeting mood. The moods of the Scarlatti Sonatas are as varied as his experiences – he travelled in Italy, England, Portugal and Spain – but they are all caught with candour. *Maestro* to the Infanta Maria Barbara at Lisbon, he accompanied her to Madrid when she married King Fernando VI. Scarlatti is more Spanish than Italian in his Sonatas. In them we hear the *flamenco*-guitar, the horse-riding of the *zapateado*, echoes of the Moorish music, Don Quixote's sigh and Sancho Panza's chuckle. His rhythm suggests the deportment and alacrity of the *torero*. His technique is innovatory. He ubiquitously crosses hands. His dissonance fairly crackles with life. His treatment of dissonance is a major exception to the generalizations made in Chapter 2. His harmonies confound people who think that only 'modern' music is dissonant. But Domenico Scarlatti's dissonances are conceived in terms of the plangency of the harpsichord, not for the percussion of the modern grand piano. Here is an example from no. XXI in the Kirkpatrick edition (Schirmer):

Domenico Scarlatti has *duende*. Read Garcia Lorca's lecture on the *duende*. He says 'all that has dark sounds has *duende*. The *duende* is not in the throat; the *duende* surges up from the soles of the feet. Which means that it is not a matter of ability, but of real live form; of blood; of ancient culture; of creative action.' Kirkpatrick is surely right when he claims that 'Domenico Scarlatti was without question the most original keyboard composer of his century'.

At the 1966 Handel Festival in Handel's birthplace, Halle, I heard superlative performances of both Handel and Scarlatti by Kirkpatrick, who paid a visit of homage to Handel's birthhouse, Kleine Ulrich Strasse no. 37, where he played the keyboard instruments in the large collection assembled there. A contemporary caricature by one Joseph Groupy depicts Handel as a bewigged wild pig playing a positive organ, with a beer barrel for organ stool. The title is *The Charming Brute* and the caption reads:

> Strange monsters have adorned the stage,
> Not Afric's coast produces more;
> And yet no land, nor clime, nor age
> Have equalled this harmonious boar.

This Hogarthian piece of brutal wit is unfortunately an exaggeration of the aspect of Handel – the monumental – which often obscures other aspects. Berlioz is on record as saying that 'Handel must have looked a brute without his wig'. And of course, there are the stories of his throwing an opera singer out of a window in his rage at the singer's ineptitude. But there is a miniature of Handel in the Museum at Halle which reveals another aspect. It is an exquisite portrait made by Christoph Platzer in 1710, when Handel was 25. It reveals an almost feminine sensibility and a blend of melancholy and merriment that we see in the well-known portrait of Mozart by Joseph Lange. This sensibility is also in Handel's music. It is often expressed in the key of G minor, which was also a favourite key of Mozart's. The G minor Trio Sonata, for two violins or flutes or oboes and harpsichord, from the group of 6 Trio Sonatas of 1733, opens with a melody of almost Mozartian tenderness:

Handel probably absorbed this kind of melody from his travels in Italy. He became friendly with Domenico Scarlatti there and once engaged in an amicable musical contest with him; Handel being judged the better organist, Scarlatti the better harpsichordist.

The broad facts of Handel's biography are well known. In Germany he was employed by George of Hanover. Handel came to London, liked it and stayed, breaking his contract. Later in 1714 George became King of England and Handel successfully played an almost operatic intrigue to reinstate himself in the royal favour. Handel became naturalized. Georg Friedrich Händel became George Frideric Handel. The Saxon became Anglo-Saxon.

George I appreciated Handel's adornment of his court music but was incapable of appreciating the music itself or of valuing its role in the development of English music. When the King's state coach first rolled through London's streets, a fat German *Frau* in the royal entourage gave the Cockney crowd a golden grin and exclaimed 'Ve komm for your goots!' Voice from the crowd: 'Ay, and for our bloody chattels!' When George II attended the royal performance of *Messiah* he stood at the *Hallelujah* Chorus. British audiences still stand up for this music. One legend has it that George II was religiously moved by the music. Another version is that he mistook it for the National Anthem.

Between 1705, when Handel produced in Hamburg his *Almira, Königen von Castilien* (libretto by Feustking), and 1742, when he produced in London his *Alceste* (libretto by Tobias Smollett), Handel wrote a total of 52 operas, a few in German, most in Italian and the last one in English. The German operas were staged in Hamburg; the later operas in Florence, Venice and London. His first oratorio, the German *Passion after the 19th Chapter of St. John* (paraphrased by Postel) was performed in Hamburg a year before his first opera. He composed a total of 33 oratorios, performed in Rome, Naples, Hamburg, one in Oxford (*Athalia*), one in Dublin (*Messiah*) but most in London. From *Messiah* onwards, that is from 1742 to 1757 he concentrated on the oratorio form, as the fashion for Italian opera waned in England. He wrote much occasional music, such as *The Royal Water Music* (performed in barges on the Thames in 1715), and *The Royal Fireworks Music* (1749); and also about 100 Italian Cantatas, anthems, arias, 18 concerti grossi, 15 organ concertos, chamber music and 17 harpsichord suites and short keyboard pieces.

Handel was a master of homophonic choral writing, master of the broad brush-stroke in sound. He thought big. His sonal edifices are monolithic, Roman. His orchestration was characterized by the sound of massed wind. Most later performances are not faithful to the sound of Handel's music as he heard it. Each successive age has rescored Handel. Mozart,

D

Mendelssohn, then Robert Franz rewrote the oratorio accompaniments. In our own day, John Tobin has been a persistent advocate of restoration of Handel's music. But it is still seldom performed with the forces Handel required. It is on record that the 'Handel Commemoration' in London, 25 years after his death, employed 26 oboes, 26 bassoons, 12 trumpets, 48 violins, etc.; that is, a ratio of fewer than 2 violins to 1 oboe. Today we hear 2 oboes to masses of strings. With such forces, Handel wrote big-boned music of direct expression with simple motives. It was surely these qualities which made Handel Beethoven's favourite composer. An example of his mastery of choral writing is the chorus, *Glory to God* from *Messiah*, which deploys the choir in dramatic antiphony:

THE BAROQUE AND ROCOCO STYLES 99

During Handel's lifetime, a movement to popularize music was astir. But it should be remembered that this movement had no relevance to the populace at large. What it meant was that, whereas music had been cultivated for centuries by royalty and the nobility, in the late 17th century the middle class began to organize musical life. About 1660 the manor of Kennington on Thames was opened as a place of public entertainment. The establishment was known as Vauxhall Gardens, named after the tenant, Mrs. Jane Vaux. The diarists Evelyn and Pepys refer to it. On 29 May 1662 Evelyn wrote: 'With my wife and the two maids and the boy took boat and to Fox-hall.' On 28 May 1667 Pepys wrote: 'By water to Fox-hall and there walked in the Spring Garden ... But to hear the nightingale and other birds, and here fiddles and there a harp, and here a Jew's trump (Jew's harp), and here laughing and there fine people walking is mighty diverting.' In 1730 Jonathan Tyers obtained the lease and built up the business. By 1736 the Gardens were open every evening in the summer. A bandstand was built and an organ installed. In 1737 Tyers commissioned Roubiliac's bust of Handel and exhibited it in the Gardens. He engaged the composer Dr. Thomas Arne, who published books of 'Vauxhall songs', such as the celebrated *Where the bee sucks*. On great occasions the throng was such that traffic was halted on London Bridge. The admission price was 2/6 – a 'bonny penny' in those days. Vauxhall had a long run, remaining open till 1859.

In the 1720's, boredom being the essence of fashion, musical London began to tire of Italian opera. The ballad opera, which was a string of popular songs and spoken dialogue, was in the ascendant. John Gay (1685–1732), a social satirist and collector of London 'street cries' ('Won't you buy my pretty lavender?' and other snatches of song) wrote the libretto of *The Beggar's Opera* and the Prussian composer Pepusch (1667–1752) arranged the music. It was a 'take-off' of Italian opera and achieved a sensational success.

Perhaps the first British merchant-patron of music was Thomas Britton (1643–1714), a London charcoal dealer. He rented rooms above his stable coal-yard in Clerkenwell, where in 1678 he established weekly concerts, sometimes graced by Handel himself. Initially the concerts were admission-free.

Later there was an annual subscription of ten shillings. It would be an erroneous romanticization to think of Britton as a pioneer of 'music for the people'. He brought music to the middle class of London. In terms of his own day he was a popularizer of music but 18th century social structure was too divided for the working class to have any place in it. Britton was the first of a line of merchant-patrons of music, which, in the 19th century flourished particularly in the North of England, notably in Manchester, Leeds and Bradford, often through Jewish philanthropy.

It is, of course, all to the good that a national art should be 'cross-fertilized' by foreign elements; and certainly not all the Jewish merchant-patrons of music were foreigners – many of these were British Jews. But the isolated island-culture of Britain, after Handel's death in 1759, developed an inferiority complex about its indigenous music. The impact of Handel was so powerful that there was a widespread suspicion, which has taken some living-down, that no Britisher could possibly equal a Continental composer. The Mendelssohn cult in Britain in the 19th century delivered another solar-plexus blow to British culture. Only in the 20th century can we see that Handel, in his superb setting of English, was an important link in the chain which extended from Purcell to Britten.

By one of those curious coincidences of history, in the very year of the birth of Handel, Scarlatti and Bach – 1685 – the English physicist, Sir Isaac Newton wrote most of his work, codifying his theory of gravity and theory of fluxions, though the theory of gravity had occupied him in the summer of 1666, when the famous observation (popularized later by Voltaire) about the falling apple may have been made, if the anecdote is not apocryphal. Only six years after Newton had codified his theories, a German theorist of music, Andreas Werckmeister (1645–1706) codified his theory of the tuning of musical instruments in his mathematical treatise, *Musikalische Temperatur* (1691). This theory consolidated the principle of tonality, which, in a way, is *gravity in sound*. The old ecclesiastic modes have a less definite, less clear-cut sound than the major/minor system of tonality. When a school child sings *do-te-la-so-fa-me-re-do*, he or she has a definite feeling of coming 'down to earth' with that final *do*, the tonic. It is a 'centre of

THE BAROQUE AND ROCOCO STYLES 101

gravity' in sound. Just as the science of physics advanced with leaps and bounds after Newton, so the range of music increased after Werckmeister. Now it is obvious that the tuning of instruments must obey certain physical laws. Before Werckmeister, tuning of keyboard instruments was based upon 'just intonation'. This was based on the theory of the Greek Aristoxemus, modified by Zarlino in Venice about 1560. Just intonation is so-called because the most important notes of the scale form natural or true intervals with the key-note, and these intervals form concords when sounded simultaneously. The other notes which did not form true intervals with the key-note (the 'centre of gravity') restricted the performance of keyboard music to certain simple keys. Keys full of flats or sharps sounded cacophonous. The Pythagorean method of tuning string instruments was in 12 perfect fifths and 7 octaves. But 12 fifths are greater than 7 octaves by a minute interval of sound, known as the 'comma maxima' or the 'Pythagorean comma.' This 'comma' is about an ⅛ of a tone. Accordingly, the Pythagorean octave comprised 5 tones and 2 semitones; not equal tones throughout. This served for monody but not for harmony. Zarlino's scale minimized the bad effects of the Pythagorean comma but produced another comma, known as the 'comma of Didymus'. Mean-tone temperament came into being in the 16th century. Temperament is a method of tuning whereby true intonation is sacrificed to attain freedom of modulation (changes of key) for keyboard instruments. In mean-tone temperament some of the fifths were so flattened that a perfect major 3rd was made out of an unpleasant-sounding interval and by the mean-tone system the octave came to have 12 notes. But here the *quinte-de-loup* or 'wolf fifth' crept in. This 'wolf' was a howling sound produced by certain chords through mean-tone temperament. The 'wolf' was kept at bay by performers only playing in certain keys. Before Werckmeister, the astronomer Kepler and the mathematician Euler experimented with new methods of tuning. Werckmeister, with one simple stroke, solved the problem by distributing the Pythagorean comma equally over the 12 fifths that make up 7 octaves. As a comma is about an ⅛ of a tone, that is, about a ¼ of a semitone, each fifth was flattened by about a forty-eighth of a semitone. Now 12 fifths equalled

7 octaves. The octave was divided into 12 equal semitones and Werckmeister's method of tuning was called 'equal temperament'. The comma was erased and the wolf put to flight.

So when the tuner tunes your piano, he actually tunes it slightly *out* of natural tuning, so that you can play a melody starting on any note you like, because all the 12 notes are equal. You can play the *National Anthem* or *The Internationale* in any key, to suit a high, medium or low voice; and it sounds the same tune in every key.

Handel did not accept Werckmeister's tuning; Bach did. Handel wrote for the mean-tone system; Bach, for equal temperament. Bach's *Well-tempered Clavier*, the famous collection of 48 Preludes and Fugues in all keys was written first as music for enlightenment and enjoyment, and, secondly, to demonstrate the new range of possibilities opened up by Werckmeister's equal temperament. Yet not even Bach was able to convert the organ-builders of his day to the new system of tuning.

Music written only a generation before Bach, say Purcell's, had frequent recourse to the ecclesiastic modes. With Bach the major/minor system of tonality was firmly established.

Bach's music has a greater range than that of any of his predecessors. There are hundreds of single, small-scale pre-Bach compositions, by Machaut, Dunstable, Josquin and others, which equal single pieces by Bach, but not one pre-Bach composer who equals Bach in his variety of forms and techniques. For that matter, very few of Bach's successors equal his range of expression, with the possible exceptions of Mozart and Shostakovich. This is not a matter of opinion. It is demonstrable. Bach's adoption of Werckmeister's equal temperament gave his music a greater range of keys than was at the disposal of any earlier composer. But his range also exceeded that of his predecessors in the variety of media for which he wrote. It spans from the simplest learning pieces for children and beginners (the *Anna Magdalena Notebook*) to the most sophisticated work of contrapuntal skill ever written (the *Art of Fugue*). Bach had the humility of greatness. He was the first composer to write music for children to perform. There is music by Mozart which children can play, but it is the music Mozart himself wrote as a child. As an adult, Mozart did not address himself to the problem of writing children's music. After Bach, Schumann was the next great composer to write for children. And after Schumann, the next examples came from Bartók, Kodály and the Soviet composers. The only form of music absent from Bach's *corpus* is opera. He had an Olympian disdain for opera and was amused by it. He would say to his son, Carl Philipp Emmanuel, 'Should we go to the Opera and hear the little tunes?' Mozart, the most universal composer, wrote in all the forms Bach employed and added opera to them. But Mozart never wrote a collection of contrapuntal pieces comparable to the *48 Preludes & Fugues*. Alone among Bach's successors, Shostakovich did that in his *24 Preludes & Fugues* (1951), though lesser composers (Bernhard Christian Weber, Hans Huber and others) have essayed it. Shostakovich has also written children's music, unlike Mozart, and opera, unlike Bach.

Because Bach has such a comprehensive range, and because his music is both detailed and consummate in craftsmanship, more space will be devoted to him here than any other composer so far.

Though Bach is a much-loved composer, there are still many people who can't understand him or who misunderstand him. There are people who are capable of enjoying a Schubert song but who say that Bach for them is 'all scales' or 'too cerebral'. And there are those who profess to like Bach because they enjoy some jazzed-up version of his music. Some music students think they are expected to admire Bach because his music is supposed to be so classical, so objective, so intellectually clever. But these are half-truths. Bach is baroque, and the baroque style is highly romantic in its monumental plasticity and range of emotion.

Schweitzer's first essay (1905) on Bach, expanded into two volumes in 1908, was entitled *Bach the musician-poet*. Some commentators on Schweitzer have accused him of 'romanticizing' Bach but this is a generalization by people who have not done the groundwork that Schweitzer did. Schweitzer's premise – that Bach associated musical motives with moods and ideas implied in the biblical paraphrases he set to music – is unassailable. He discovered eleven basic types of motive in Bach. These constitute an index or ground plan to the understanding of

Bach's music. If people who have found Bach incomprehensible or uniformly dull will bother to learn to recognize the basic motives in his music, what has been obscure will be illumined. The greatest art demands effort. You get out of it according to what you put into it. Schweitzer gives copious examples of each of Bach's motives. The following selection is limited to one example of each type.

1 The 'step' motive suggests the confident steps of faith:

or the wavering steps of doubt or weariness:

2 The motive of beatific peace:

3 The motive of noble lamentation:

or torturing grief:

THE BAROQUE AND ROCOCO STYLES

4 The motive of joy is expressed by one of these rhythms:

Ex 67 Cantata 125: Mit Fried' und Freud (the joy of the aged Simeon)

Mass in B minor: Laudamus te

5 The 'tumult' motive employs a pivotal note and expresses rage, fighting, uproar, etc.:

Ex 68 Cantata 80: Ein' feste Burg

6 The motive of exhaustion employs rests:

Ex 69 Cantata

7 The motive of solemnity and majesty uses the rhythm

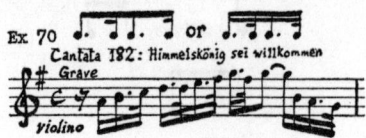

8 The motive of violent passions, generally grievous but sometimes joyful, has the rhythm

9 The motive of peaceful joy is realized in the rhythm

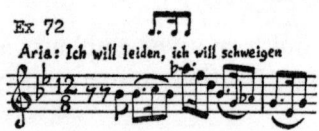

10 The motive of terror is expressed in tremolo:

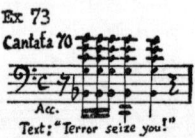

THE BAROQUE AND ROCOCO STYLES

11 The 'sighing' motive has two forms:
(a) realistic:

(b) idealistic:

Schweitzer also demonstrates the co-operation of motives in Bach, such as the expression of terror and joy in the *Christmas Oratorio*, when Herod asks the Magi: 'Why should you fear? Should you not rejoice?'

It is not only in Bach's word-setting that he employs these motival associations of ideas; he also carries them over into his purely instrumental music, even in its simpler forms. The E major *Two-part Invention* expresses torturing grief turned to joy:

Readers wishing to explore further examples might listen to the following from Book I of the '48'. Fugue 1 – the step motive: faith. Fugue 2 – the motive of joy: dancing for joy. Fugue 5: the motive of solemnity and majesty. Prelude 8: the motive of grief.

In support of the contention that Bach's music is baroque and therefore romantic, there are passages from his music which suggest even Chopin, as does this phrase from Prelude 9 of the '48':

Ex 78 [Allegretto]

The textbook idea that classical music was composed in the 18th century, romantic in the 19th and modern music in the 20th century is a too facile generalization. Bach is anticipatory of much that came later but is also connected with his predecessors. He was a great conservative. His sons called him 'the old periwig'. In the second half of the 20th century, when we are witnessing exhibitions of artists trying to outvie each other in the fabrication of sensationalism, it is salutary to realize that the general features of Bach's contrapuntal style were identical with the style of composers writing two centuries before him. An example of this is the comparison of the following *coda* from *Antonio de Cabezón's Prelude in the Dorian mode* (Cabezón lived two centuries before Bach) and the coda of Bach's Fugue 5 from Book 2 of the '48':

Ex 79 Cabezón

THE BAROQUE AND ROCOCO STYLES

This comparison suggests a question: what would the fashionable western music critics of 1970 say of a contemporary composer who brought out a composition written in the style of a composer of 1770? They would dismiss him with contempt. But they don't dismiss Bach because he wrote this fugal coda in the style of Cabezón. It happened ages ago. The dead are safe. But someone may ask: haven't events accelerated much more between 1770 and 1970 than they did between 1560 (Cabezón's death) and 1750 (Bach's death)? Yes, but this is irrelevant to Cabezón and Bach and any composer in any period – including the present – who is concerned with the stuff of music, with its essence, which is the human voice, a higher form of human speech. The basic inflexions of the articulation of human emotion are constant, and so are the musical intonations which capture them.

Bach's art was concerned with what is basic to music, and he refined on this basis. His gift as a contrapuntist was consummate. He could improvise a fugue in 6 voices, as he did on his visit to Frederick the Great. This ability presupposes ability to organize combinations of melodies with sovereign control, seeing – or, rather, hearing – ahead. But if there was a commanding sweep to his polyphony, his harmony evinced attention to detail. In the chorales (German hymn tunes with interesting melodies for every voice) particular chords or cadences are suggested by ideas in the text. The *Saint Matthew Passion* includes different harmonizations of the same tune. Compare the following quotations:

The 'crown of thorns' imagery in the first setting determines the choice of the piercing chord marked by the asterisk. The final cadence of this first setting glorifies Christ's name by the short melisma in the tenor part and by forthright harmony. By contrast, the second setting is transposed to a lower key, in keeping with the subdued tone of the subject of death. Also the final cadence of this version calmly sinks into oblivion – an entirely different treatment from the cadence of glorification.

An incidental point while dealing with the chorale: the pause at the end of the phrase originated in the necessity for the minister to intone the words of the consequent line for the benefit of the mainly illiterate congregation. By softly improvising music during these pauses, the chorale-prelude was evolved. Samuel Scheidt (1587–1654) was one of the pioneers of the chorale-prelude and the father of German organ music. Though none of Scheidt's chorale-preludes is extant, his *Tablature Book* of 100 chorale harmonizations (1650) has come down to us. Other masters of the chorale-prelude who immediately preceded Bach were the Germans, Pachelbel and Bohm, and the Dane, Buxtehude, who settled in North Germany.

Bach, unlike Handel, did not call for large orchestral forces. It is documented that he wanted three instruments to each string part of his *Brandenburg Concerto no. 3* – a ratio generally overlooked today.

With characteristic modesty and uncharacteristic untruth, Bach once said that anyone could achieve what he had done, if they would work as hard. As a young boy he was forced to independence by the death of his parents and lack of sympathy from his elder brother, who acted as his guardian. He pursued knowledge the hard way – the best way. He copied out reams of music, ultimately impairing his sight. He walked miles to hear celebrated organists perform. In theory, modern aids to study – state grants, rapid photocopying and tape recording of study material and so on – should give the modern music student a big start on Bach's studentship. In practice, modern methods encourage laziness. A little money but no effort is required to photocopy music. Files of photocopies may be impressive critical apparatus but often go unread. Copying music by hand forces you to read it: if you don't, you make a slip. Bach worked.

The chronicle of Bach's life is simply a handful of place-names and dates and ordinary appointments. There is no outward show. All the splendour is in the work. His forebears were musical. The miller, old Viet Bach, played the fiddle. Johann Sebastian Bach – the great Bach – was born in Eisenach, East Germany. He held church appointments in Arnstadt and Mühlhausen, 1704–7; court posts at Weimar, 1708–17, and Cöthen, 1717–23; and taught school and was organist at St. Thomas's in Leipzig from 1723 to his death in 1750. His music was written to serve the particular community in which he worked: cantatas, passions and organ music for the churches, instrumental and orchestral music for the courts. As an organist he was expected to accompany the congregational hymn-singing discreetly. He didn't. As a school-teacher, he was expected to be a disciplinarian. He wasn't. Wherever he went there were frictions, rows. Not because he was 'difficult'. Because people could not see him as he was – one of the few supreme geniuses in the history of mankind. It was to be expected.

Bach and Handel are complementary opposites, however similar their work may appear superficially. They both came from eastern Germany but never met. They were both operated upon by the same oculist: Handel successfully, Bach unsuccessfully. Both went blind, Bach first. Handel travelled much, Bach little. Bach married twice and had twenty children; Handel remained a bachelor. Handel's music is at its greatest in large-scale harmony; Bach's in monumental polyphony, though they both worked in a mainly contrapuntal era. Handel's music has the massed effect of Rubens's paintings; Bach's the controlled draughtsmanship of Dürer. Handel was a man of the world, Bach a world of a man.

Bach was a Protestant, yet he composed the Catholic *Mass in B minor*, one of his supreme achievements.

A mathematics of beauty lay behind Bach's music. This connects him with a few of his contemporaries, who were great thinkers in other fields. The philosophies of Spinoza, Descartes and Leibniz all had a mathematical basis. Leibniz unwittingly wrote the most apt comment on Bach in his dictum: *Musica est exercitium occultum nescientis animi* (Music is a mysterious mathematics of the soul unconscious of its calculation.)

Bach's *Goldberg Variations* exploit the device of canon at every interval. His last work, *The Art of Fugue*, explores every aspect of fugue. The patient labour demanded by the creation (and appreciation) of such works might be compared to the work of another contemporary of Bach: the Swedish botanist, Karl von Linné (*Linneaus*), who classified flowers by their Latin names. Latin names are also employed in the study of fugue. The first 'voice' (whether human or instrumental) is called the *dux* (leader); the answering or following voice, the *comes*. But if we have any imagination, we smell the scents of the flowers as we turn the pages of Linné's tome; and, if we have musicality, we hear the sounding soul coming through the mathematical microcosm of Bach's music.

A word about fugue. We use the word when we say *tempus fugit* – 'time flies'. A fugue is a flight of voices. It can be as lovely as a flight of birds. It is based on a musical subject, as a sermon is based on a text. Different voices 'discourse' on the subject. 'Voice' here means a single strand of melody, whether sung or played. And there are episodes, passages where the subject does not occur; this makes variety. There are three sections to a fugue: the exposition of the subject in all the voices; the middle section or development; and the final section. Fugue is the most intellectual form of music. That statement need not be scarifying to people who find pleasure in a game of chess. Second-rate fugues are nothing but little games in sound. A double fugue is based on two subjects; triple fugue on three subjects, and so on. Bach's finest fugues (say the C sharp minor or E flat minor from Book I of the '48') are music of profoundly human, emotional content.

Bach dwarfs all other composers working in Germany at that time, though they included some fine composers such as Reinhard Keiser, Johann Mattheson and Georg Philipp Telemann.

Towards the end of Bach's life, the influence of French music began to be felt in German music. The German baroque style burgeoned through Italian influence; now the German rococo style became the fashion, following French models.

To trace the development of rococo music, we must go back to the music of the founder of the French school of harpsichordists, the 'clavecinists', Jean Champion Chambonnières (1602–72). His first book of pieces (1670) was the first to tabulate *agréments* (ornaments). His characteristic form was to write a dance movement which itself was liberally sprinkled with ornaments (what folk-singers call 'twiddly bits') and then write a variation called a *double* in which the ornaments proliferated. Chambonnières taught the three Couperin brothers, one of whom, Charles, was the father of François Couperin, called *'le Grand'* (1668–1733). The number of Couperins is legion, like the Bachs; but just as we speak of Johann Sebastian Bach, simply as Bach, when we speak of Couperin we mean François Couperin.

The rococo element in Couperin's music reflected the masquerades and pastorals painted by Watteau in his *fêtes galantes*. Though he wrote music for media other than the harpsichord, including church music, his harpsichord music is his best work. Wanda Landowska called him 'the Chopin of the harpsichord.' This epithet seems particularly appropriate after the experience of hearing the piano recordings made by Paderewski of Couperin's *La Bandoline* and *Le Carillon de Cythère* (recordings admired by Landowska herself). Landowska also writes of Couperin's simplicity of character ('a sort of *bourgeois gentilhomme*') and admonishes us not to think that his music depicts only courtly manners. She describes his low-ceilinged dwelling with its peasant garden and finds there, rather than at Versailles, the intimate atmosphere of his music. His main harpsichord works were the *ordres*, or suites. (Another name for suite was 'lesson', the term used by Purcell.) The *Passacaille* from the 8th *Ordre* is probably Couperin's finest work.

Jean Phillipe Rameau (1683-1764) ranged wider than Couperin yet achieved nothing as polished. They were opposites: Couperin, contented with the corner of beauty he had discovered, a simple hedonist with the sensualist's lips and soft hands; Rameau, restless, enquiring, industrious, with the thin lips of the ascetic and bony hands always searching for something beyond his grasp. His work is the musical counterpart of the Enlightenment, the socio-political trend in the 18th century French philosophy which was directed towards correcting the shortcomings of existing society and towards changing its morals and manners by the dissemination of rationality, justice and science. Its chief theorists were Voltaire, Rousseau and Montesquieu. Rameau's work as a theorist of music ran parallel to the philosophical writings of those compatriots and contemporaries of his. In his *Traité de l'harmonie* (1722) he discovered the law of inversion of chords. Before this discovery, the following chords were considered as different harmonies:

THE BAROQUE AND ROCOCO STYLES 115

Rameau saw that they were three forms of the same chord: the root chord, the first inversion and the second inversion. Rameau wrote many operas, much theatre music and a fair corpus of keyboard music. His masterpiece was the opera *Castor et Pollux* (1737). He extended the operatic overture, introduced woodwind solos in orchestration, developed the syllabic style of word-setting and enlivened ballet both by reference to indigenous peasant dances and by exotic touches such as the music in *Les Sauvages*, inspired by two Louisianan Red Indians whose dancing he had witnessed at the Italian Theatre in Paris in 1725. His harpsichord music constitutes, as Landowska expressed it, 'a page of living history from the reign of Louis XV'.

One of the chief philosophers of the Enlightenment, Jean Jacques Rousseau (1712–78), was also a composer, as well as a rediscoverer of nature and the noble savage and theorist of liberal pedagogy and the 'social contract' which was a seminal influence on the French Revolution. At Fontainebleu in 1752 he brought out his operetta *Le Devin du village* ('The Village Soothsayer') which enjoyed immense popularity and established the new *genre* of the peasant pastoral, breaking away from the heroic myth of the *tragédie lyrique*. Many composers wrote this type of operetta and later even Mozart wrote an example of it in his *Bastien et Bastienne*. Rousseau also contributed articles on music (not very accurate) to the Encyclopedia, the depository of Enlightenment knowledge (*L'Encyclopédie, ou Dictionnaire Raisonné des Sciences, des Arts et des Métiers*, edited by Diderot and D'Alembert, 1751–80). And Rousseau engaged in the polemics with which 18th century French musical life was riddled. In the famous *guerre des buffons* ('the war of the buffonists') he espoused the side of the buffonists, the supporters of the Italian *opera buffa* (comic opera) against the school of French opera.

This was a period of many such 'wars', among them that of the Gluckists and the Piccinists. Though these battles have a distant rumble in modern ears, they were taken very seriously in their time. Niccola Piccini (1728–1800) was a Neapolitan composer who settled in Paris and took the French capital by storm. His *La Cecchina* (1760) was the most popular *opera buffa* ever composed: wines, inns, shops and villas were named after it. His operas were display-cabinets for arias, aviaries for human canaries. Christoph Willibald Gluck (1714–87), on the other hand, reinstated the importance of declamation in French opera and did some hard thinking about the nature of opera, distilled in the preface to his *Alceste* (1767). Gluck was born in the Upper Palatinate and brought up in Bohemia, Prague and Vienna, where his operas were first produced. As Paris had become the opera centre of Europe, he determined to conquer it and wrote French operas which ultimately triumphed over the Parisian taste for superficial entertainment. His *Orphée et Euridice* (1774) – yet another treatment of the subject of the first opera – still holds the boards, and the recording by Kathleen Ferrier of Orpheus's Lament is cherished by music lovers who are not necessarily opera lovers. Gluck is an important landmark in operatic reform who stands mid-way between Peri, the founder of opera, and Wagner, the creator of the music-drama. Gluck also pioneered orchestral reforms. He took the harpsichord continuo (continuous background harmonic filling-in) out of the orchestra and introduced the harp, clarinets and trombones. He purified his melody of excessive ornamentation and abjured his singers to banish the vanity of embellishment. He spent his last years in Vienna, and, in the noble simplicity of his style he anticipates the music of the Viennese classics, Haydn, Mozart and Beethoven.

Meanwhile in Germany four of Bach's sons pursued careers as composers. Wilhelm Friedmann (1710–84) was the eldest son of Bach's first marriage, a wayward genius frustrated by being heir to an illustrious father. His indolence allowed only intermittent work and often made him prefer improvisation to composition. Carl Philipp Emmanuel (1714–88) was Bach's second son by his first marriage. He was an industrious composer and theorist of piano technique who was *Kappelmeister* to Frederick the Great. Johann Christoph Friedrich (1732–95), was the eldest surviving son of Bach's second marriage, a composer of choral and chamber music more than of keyboard music; and Johann Christian (1735–82), was the youngest son of Bach's second marriage. A friend of Mozart, he is called 'the London Bach', because he lived his last years and died in London; a composer of light operas, concertos and

THE BAROQUE AND ROCOCO STYLES 117

symphonies and some keyboard music which never attempts more than moderate technical difficulties. Carl Philipp Emmanuel Bach is generally called 'the father of sonata form' but there are examples of bi-thematic sonata form in the work of earlier composers, notably in Giovanni-Battista Somis (1676–1763), a pupil of Corelli and Vivaldi. Nevertheless, C. P. E. Bach was the main influence on Haydn's development of sonata form. Though the form of C. P. E. Bach's works was of a Germanic mould, there was sometimes a dichotomy between that form and its content which had a tendency towards French expression, sometimes not unlike Couperin. This influence may even be read into some of the titles of his short keyboard pieces such as *Les langueurs tendres* (1761). In Germany the French rococo style became known as the galant style or *galanterie*.

French influence dominated the German courts. French was their official language. Frederick the Great's Palace at Potsdam was named 'Sans Souci' ('Care-free') and Frederick himself cultivated French wind music, playing and composing for the flute. Mannheim was another centre where French culture fertilized Teutonic music. This main port of the upper Rhine, the chief emporium for south Germany, was taken and retaken five times during the Thirty Years' War and fell to the French in 1688 and again in 1794. Due to ecclesiastic disputes, the Elector Palatine Carl Philip transferred his residence from Heidelberg to Mannheim in 1720. It remained the capital of the Palatinate for over sixty years and flourished particularly under the Elector Carl Theodor. Under him the Mannheim Orchestra, conducted by the Czech Jan Vaclav Stamic or, in Germanized form, Johann Stamitz (1717–51), became the leading orchestra in Europe. Stamic trained his musicians individually and in sectional group-rehearsal as well as in *tutti* (full ensemble). The result was that their 'attack' and precision of ensemble eclipsed anything else in Europe at that time. The orchestral personnel included musicians from Austria, Bohemia and Italy. Stamic sojourned in France and imported clarinets from Paris for use in the Mannheim Orchestra. The music of the Court of Mannheim was stylistically midway between the *galant* style and the classical style of the Viennese school. One of its characteristic features, an opening 'broken chord' figure played in unison and octaves by the full orchestra – a kind of 'opening gambit' probably originating in Stamic's rehearsal routine of a preliminary test of tuning – became known as the 'Mannheim rocket'. Some form of it is frequently found at the opening of works by the Viennese classical composers. Three examples are appended, one each from Haydn, Mozart and Beethoven:

Ex 82 Haydn: Minuet from 'The Queen' Symphony
Mozart: 1st mvt, Symphony K.134
Beethoven: 1st mvt, Sonata Op. 2, no. 1

12 The Viennese Classics

The reader who has persisted thus far will have noticed that we have reached the eighteenth century and music has been almost entirely organized by or for royalty, nobles, and the like; and the composers have mainly come from the middle class or the aristocracy. The recalcitrance of aristocratic power may be seen in the Hapsburg dynasty, which stretched from 1273 to 1918. But with the Viennese Classics – Haydn, Mozart, Beethoven and Schubert – we see how composers are gradually becoming more democratic. They were Viennese by residence; alone of their number, Schubert was born in a suburb of Vienna. Haydn was a Croatian peasant, Mozart an upper middle-class Salzburger, Beethoven a lower middle-class Rhinelander of Walloon-Flemish stock, Schubert a lower middle-class Austrian of Silesian peasant stock. They were all employed by the aristocracy and all reacted differently to their employers. Haydn exercised humour and cajoled Prince Esterhazy into granting fairer working conditions for his orchestra. Mozart was forced to enter the residence of his employer, the Archbishop Hieronymus of Salzburg, by the tradesman's entrance and, when Mozart requested a wage-rise, the Archbishop abused him and the valet literally kicked him out. When Beethoven's patrons didn't pay up punctually, he let them know in blunt language, treating them as equals or inferiors. Schubert had a gentler character than Beethoven, yet was aware of the dilemma of the artist in bourgeois society. He abandoned employment as a young schoolmaster to work freelance. Exploited by publishers, he depended on the charity of friends. He is reported to have told a friend, over a glass of punch,

'The state should support me in order that I might compose free from care.'

Analysis of social class is fundamental to appreciation of the differences between the kind of music the Viennese classics wrote.

Haydn sometimes employed the irregular phrase-lengths of 5 bars instead of 4, 9 instead of 8, found in Croatian folk dances. Mozart on the other hand, in his preference for regularity of phrase-length, reflected the order of the court life and its dances with which he grew up. Beethoven punctuated regular rhythms by irregular syncopations, symbolic of the protesting spirit of the brusque Bonn man who invaded polite Viennese society; and Schubert emulated his musical manner, if not his rough manners.

Haydn and Schubert, whose families preserved peasant traditions, both sometimes used folk songs or folk song types of melody. Mozart and Beethoven, whose upbringing was urban, did not naturally refer to folk song, though Beethoven arranged folk song when commissioned to do – and his original works do quote a few German folk songs. Mozart's music has little of nature in it, except that some of his *divertimenti* (such things as *Eine kleine Nachtmusik*) were meant to be performed in the open air, and, in that setting, have a frail gaiety as transient as life. Haydn's music, when not designed for courtly diversion, is full of the songs and dances of open air folk and has gypsy abandon; Beethoven's music is the testament of a passionate pantheist; and Schubert's is rich in reminiscences of country excursions.

Those four composers wrote in all the forms of music – oratorio, mass, opera, ballet, song, quartet, concerto, symphony; but let us consider how they wrote for the voice, as an index to the human content of their music. Haydn's oratorio *The Creation* sings with joy and nobility of the simple faith of a merry heart. Mozart's three greatest operas, *Figaro*, *Don Giovanni* and *The Magic Flute*, sing of the fun and pathos of life's intrigues; but they sing of these things at a certain distance, as it were, for Mozart has such mastery that he can identify himself with his operatic characters and yet remain apart by writing music of almost superhuman perfection for situations of all-too-human imperfection. Beethoven was the first to use voices in a symphony – the Ninth. This inspired use of voices bursting through the traditionally exclusive orchestral form of the symphony, is itself a symbol of Beethoven's will to break barriers by asserting human rights. And Schubert poured out his humanity in music by writing over 600 songs.

Haydn, the peasant, preferred the double-reed 'open air' tone of the oboe to the single-reed tone of the clarinet. Mozart, the erstwhile prodigy at court, preferred the smooth 'aristocratic' tone of the clarinet to the oboe (his own description of the Mannheim orchestra's clarinets was 'lordly'). Beethoven, the rebel, mixed single and double reed-tone and added to them a more forceful deployment of brass than Haydn or Mozart used, in order to emphasize the exhortatory, political content of his message. And Schubert emulated Beethoven in this.

The relationship between class distinction and death was a drastic one at the beginning of the 19th century. It can be summed up in the sentence: the poor died younger than the rich. It would be incorrect to assume that, because Haydn was born a peasant, he remained poor; or that because Beethoven was born in the lower middle-class, he lived in poverty. Both Haydn and Beethoven were well-off: Haydn through the exercise of shrewd humour, Beethoven through the roughness of his tongue; and both worked hard. Mozart and Schubert worked possibly even harder, but they lacked Haydn's shrewdness and Beethoven's toughness. Mozart, after a childhood in the courts of Europe, lived in penury and went to a pauper's grave. Schubert was paid in pennies for the world's greatest songs. The inventory of his effects drawn up after his death included his manuscripts, described as 'old music, valued at 8s 6d'. Haydn died at 77, Beethoven at 57, Mozart at 35 and Schubert at 31.

The most significant development in the music of the Viennese classics, as compared with previous music, is the growth of the symphony. This evolved from the 18th century dance suite, which comprised such dances as the allemande, a sober German dance in 4-beat rhythm; the sarabande, a stately Spanish dance of Saracen origin in 3-beat rhythm; the gavotte, a good humoured French dance originating in the Gap country of Dauphiné, in 4-beat rhythm, each phrase beginning on a third beat; the musette, a companion piece to the gavotte, a kind of 'bagpipe'-gavotte over a drone bass; the bourrée, a French or Spanish dance, a more rapid gavotte, with each phrase beginning on the 4th beat; the minuet, a French court dance of mincing steps in 3-beat rhythm; the courante, a rapid French 'running' dance in 3-beat rhythm and the gigue, a dance originally to a fiddle – the word derives from the German word for fiddle, *Geige* – in 2, 3 or 4-beat rhythm, each beat subdivided into three. Most of these dances got into the court musicians' gallery by the tradesman's entrance, that is, from the dances of the people. The title of one of the oldest dances, the passacaglia, is itself proof of its popular origin, for the word 'passacaglia' derives from the Spanish meaning to pace or step or dance on the street. The passacaglia traditionally is in 3-beat rhythm, with a characteristic syncopation (off-main-beat stress) on the second beat which derived from the stamp of the foot in the dance. It also has a repeated bass part (a 'ground bass') over which variations are woven, like the weaving in and out of dance sets and strings of songs, while the street musicians kept a constant background going. Later the passacaglia entered the court and became a highly sophisticated form of music-making.

In their original folk forms all these dances we have mentioned, and others too, were associated with work, or holiday from work, and the community participated. When these dances were absorbed into court music, they were no longer associated with work but with leisure. What had been active with the people became passive with the courtiers. Lusty joy became melancholy pleasure. Instead of everybody making music, now only a few made it and others listened or chatted through it. Gradually, dance suites were divorced from dancing and composed simply to be heard without dancing. The word 'suite', incidentally, is applied to music to mean a group of homogeneous yet contrasted pieces, just as it is applied to a suite of furniture. The separate movements of the 18th century dance suite became the sonata, an instrumental piece in different movements, one of which is written in sonata form. When a sonata was written for three or more instruments, it took the name of the number of instruments employed: trio, quartet and so on. When a sonata was written for orchestra it was called a symphony. When it was written for solo instrument and orchestra, it was called a concerto.

Symphony is the 'book of life' in the sense in which D. H. Lawrence said the novel was. Symphony is mankind in music. It evolved during the period which led to the French Revolution. One of the first symphonists was a Walloon composer François-Joseph Gossec (1734–1829), whose first Symphony is dated 1753 – six years before Haydn's first Symphony, though Haydn is often called 'the father of the symphony'. Gossec identified himself with the cause of the French Revolution and composed music honouring it. With the 18th century dance suite, street music, village music and country music were made to do service in royal courts. With the symphony, the music which the court had purloined from the country was recaptured for the people and brought out again into the open to be heard by everybody instead of the few. Beethoven in his first Symphony even swept the minuet out of court by accelerating it beyond the confined choreography of whalebone hoops and high heels.

The mature Beethoven's musical thinking was imbued with symphonic form. I say 'mature Beethoven' because he had a struggle to forge his musical language – which was all to the good, because struggle is the stuff of symphony. He struggled, too, against deafness, becoming totally deaf in his maturity. His thought was so symphonic that he could make even a short song a miniature symphonic movement. He did this in the song *Creation's Hymn*, which is found in many school song books. Sonata form, or first movement form, is illustrated most often from sonatas or symphonies. This Beethoven song is chosen as the most succinct illustration of sonata form. After a brief introduction of two loud chords, each repeated, the first subject appears:

It consists of trumpet-like leaps. The words tell of the vastness of the cosmos. The second subject contrasts with it:

Ex 84

It consists of softly repeated monotones. Here the words tell of the earth and the striving of man. These two subjects are then developed:

Ex 85

This music begins like the first subject but continues like the second subject. Man is brought into ratio with the cosmos. Finally, to make his meaning clear, Beethoven reminds us of his two subjects by repeating them; only, he doesn't repeat the second subject exactly — he raises it, as though to show that by thought and action about mankind and the universe, man increases his stature:

Ex 86

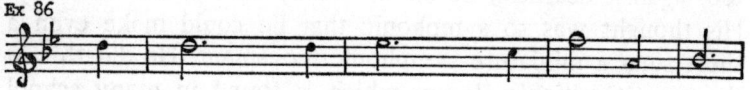

Theorists have given names to the three main parts of sonata form. The first part, comprising the two subjects, is called the exposition; that is, the subjects are exposed, the 'cards put on the table'. The second part is called the development; the third part, the recapitulation. Sonata form is music made in the image of man, because tripartite structure is basic to human anatomy. It is seen in the head, trunk and limbs. And each part of the body has three subdivisions: forehead, nose and chin; the three phalanxes of the fingers, and so on.

Sonata form has been compared to the heroic type of novel. The two contrasting subjects are like the hero and heroine; the development is the unravelling of the plot, and the recapitulation is the drawing together of the threads of the story, the conclusion. But, as the sonata, quartet, symphony or concerto is in multiple movements, the comparison would have to be with a novel in more than one volume. This comparison between sonata form and novel is very simple but will bear scrutiny. For instance, though the comparison of the two subjects to the hero and heroine sounds naive, very often the first subject is virile and laconic and the second subject is feminine and lyrical – think of Beethoven's Fifth, for example with its first subject:

and its second subject:

Main occurrences in sonata form result from harmonic/rhythmic relationships which theorists call tonality. Tovey described tonality as 'perspective' in sound. Changes in melodic inflections are indicated by signs (sharps, flats, naturals) before the printed notes. In the above examples from *Creation's Hymn* there was no change in inflection in the first subject, but there was a change in the last note of the example from the second subject and there were more changes in the excerpt from the development. These inflectional changes in the melody register changes at a deeper harmonic level, just as a seismograph records subterranean disturbances. The disturbances registered in music are the volcanic eruptions of the heart and mind of genius. For the music of Beethoven, that is not too dramatic a metaphor, Haydn foreshadowed Beethoven's use of tonality. Haydn's dates are 1732–1809; Beethoven's, 1770–1827. The most outstanding example of this foreshadowing occurs in Haydn's Piano Sonata in E flat, the longest and greatest sonata he wrote. Ultimately, Haydn's and Beethoven's use of tonality can only be understood by listening to the music. Verbally, it is demonstrable only by technical language.

The first movement of Haydn's Sonata in E flat is, as the title tells us, in E flat; that is, E flat is its 'centre of gravity'. The development section of the first movement shifts to other keys, including E major. On the piano keyboard, this is only a small shift from a black key to the next higher white key. But the paradox is that this small step represents a big step in terms of harmony and tonality. It is a change which implies deep perspective. The perspective is even deepened when Haydn, having referred to E major in the first movement, takes this key as the tonality of the second movement. It is interesting to observe how he solves the problem of 'getting back home' to E flat major. He does this by beginning the *finale* on one note, a gentle tapping on the note G. After the last chord of the previous movement (a chord of E major), the tapping on the note G sounds as if the finale is beginning in E minor; for that note G belongs to the chord of E minor, which, of course, is a related chord to E major. But the note G is also found in the chord of E flat. So Haydn has alighted upon an ambiguity of sound – a kind of pun in music – by which he is able to switch us back home in no time. Beethoven developed this kind of perspective in sound and with it went a deepening of human content.

In his first two symphonies, Beethoven made the development section of his sonata form much longer than was Haydn's or Mozart's practice. Mozart in particular wrote short development sections, preferring to concentrate and crystallize rather than expand. The nature of Mozart's gift – probably the most phenomenal in the history of music – was almost superhuman. It seemed to enable him to stand outside of struggle over material. This made for concision instead of expansion. Beethoven, on the other hand, needed to expand form in order to struggle with his material (and with himself). A long development section is not enough in the first movement of his third symphony, the 'Eroica': he makes the coda to the movement *another* development section. In his fifth Symphony, even one whole movement is no longer adequate space for development. He develops the famous opening 'fate-knocking-at-the-door' motive not only in the first movement but also in the third and fourth movements, where its rhythm re-appears in monotone.

Beethoven's ninth and last Symphony (1824) exemplifies not only awesome perspectives in sound but a large concept of *historical* perspective. It opens with an atavistic evocation of ancient music, the only harmony of the first 16 bars being the open 'bagpipe' fifth; and it closes with a hymn to the joy of future world democracy. Beethoven, born in 1770, was 19 when the French Revolution erupted. It is well known that he dedicated his 'Eroica' Symphony to Napoleon in 1804, but tore off the dedication when he realized that Napoleon had become a dictator instead of a liberator. Beethoven lived to see his ideal of democracy caricatured. But he did not lose hope in its ultimate triumph.

If Beethoven could on occasion make a miniature symphonic movement out of a song, Schubert made his symphonies grand songs. Schubert is the greatest melodist in western music. That is not a matter of opinion but demonstrable. His melody has a greater variety of types than those of any other composer, and a correspondingly great variety of expression and psychology. If you study folksong of a specific country, you will find that each region of the country has its characteristic type of melody. In Schubert's melody, the work of one man embraces such different types of melody as are found in different regions of a country, as the products of different types of people. Indeed, his music includes melodic types from four different cultures: Silesia (his father's home); Prussia, the Northern boundary of Silesia; Hungary, the southern boundary of Silesia; and Austria, where Schubert himself lived.

Schubert's dynamic range did not equal Beethoven's at the level of the greatest volume and density of sound, but it excelled it at the lowest level. Beethoven had two dynamic hallmarks: the *subito sforzato* (sudden forced accentuation) and the *subito piano* (a sudden drop to quiet sound). Schubert's *sforzato* did not urge his music forward with the kinetic propulsion of Beethoven, but in the music of Schubert's last years, Beethoven's *subito piano* was extended into characteristic silences significantly placed in the music. The effect of Beethoven's sudden drop to quiet tone was to emphasize changes of tonality and to make the perspective of tonality clearer by a dynamic sense of 'nearness' and 'distance'. His *subito piano* affords us glimpses of the valley of the shadow, sudden glimpses caught in the midst of life. But with Schubert's silences we walk with him in the valley of the shadow. Schubert's last music is a song of life sung at death's gate. Though his song cycle *Die Winterreise* (Winter Journey) contains music of frozen, numb emotion, other music written in his last year says 'yes' to life and is full of fragrance and the sweetness of children's smiles.

Not only a supreme melodist, Schubert is also a great harmonist. Harmonies darken and brighten his melodies like cloud and sun scudding over a cornfield. He has 'secret', endearing harmonies, like words from a diary or in a love-letter. As Liszt so truly said of him, he is 'the most poetic of all composers'. As a poet in sound, only Chopin approaches him.

His industry may even be compared to Mozart's. To facilitate comparison, let us give their dates: Mozart, 1756–91; Schubert, 1797–1828. Mozart began composing at 5 and died at 35: a composing life of 30 years. Schubert's first extant work dates from his 16th year and he died at 31: a composing life of 15 years. The number of compositions in the Köchel catalogue of Mozart's work is 626. The number of compositions in the Deutsch catalogue of Schubert's work is 960. Though Schubert's output includes many songs, these were, in most cases, not minor works but carefully worked out compositions with important and sometimes even symphonic piano parts. Schubert's output is all the more prodigious when it is realized that, whereas many of Mozart's works were written in a kind of musical 'shorthand' which he intended the performer to fill in, Schubert's were written out in detail.

Mozart is the greatest stylist of all composers. His output includes music in the style of Bach (the Fantasy in F minor for mechanical organ, K.608), in the style of Handel (the Fugue in C for piano, K.394) and countless pieces in the French or in the Italian manner. He also sometimes foreshadows Beethoven (compare the C minor Piano Concertos of both composers). In dissonance Mozart even foreshadows later composers than Beethoven, as in the opening of the 'Dissonance' Quartet, K.465:

or in the Minuet for piano, K.355

The 20th century French composer Darius Milhaud even unearthed a Schoenbergian twelve note series in the statue scene from Mozart's *Don Giovanni*:

Mozart is the kind of unique phenomenon in music that Leonardo is as a Renaissance universal thinker or Einstein in modern physics. He defies description. He produces a near-miracle like the 'Jupiter' Symphony and yet remains child-like. Busoni said some of the truest things about Mozart in the thirty-five Mozart aphorisms he wrote in 1906, from which the following quotations are selected.

> His smile is not the diplomat's or the actor's but that of a pure soul – and yet worldly-wise.
> He is temperamental without nervousness, idealist without vagueness, realist without ugliness.
> Serene merriment is his salient characteristic.
> In the most tragic situation he can still joke; in the most lighthearted he can still frown philosophically.
> His feeling for form is almost superhuman.
> He has the freshness of youth and the wisdom of age; neither ancient nor modern, he has been buried yet lives.
> His transfigured human smile still radiates to us...

Writing in his last years on the nature of music, Busoni avers that Mozart demonstrates the fundamental unity of all music because with him 'every opera is a symphonic score, every quartet a distillation of an operatic scene'.

Writing of Mozart's opera, *The Marriage of Figaro*, E. J. Dent said: 'There can be no doubt that the political sympathies of both Da Ponte (the librettist) and Mozart were with the ideas that found vent in Paris in 1789 and that they deliberately chose this unusual subject for their opera with a view to popular success. (The original Beaumarchais comedy from which *Figaro* was adapted has often been called 'the prologue to the French Revolution'.) It may be pointed out here that their two subsequent operas, *Don Giovanni* and *Cosí fan Tutte*, both make fun of the privileged classes and present them in ridiculous situations, while Mozart's last opera, *The Magic Flute*, written to German words for a humbler type of audience, bids a definite farewell to the ideas of the eighteenth century and opens the door to the doctrines of Liberty, Equality and Fraternity.' (Preface to Dent's translation of Da Ponte's libretto of *Figaro*.)

THE VIENNESE CLASSICS

But though there is a greater range of style and idea in Mozart than in any other composer, there is nowhere in his work the true folk ethos that is found in Schubert. The ethos of *The Magic Flute* is a pantomime of folklore. The trio of the scherzo of Schubert's Piano Sonata in A minor (Deutsch 845) on the other hand contains a Hungarian-type pentatonic folk melody (incidentally, a scherzo is a quick 'joke' of a piece – the word means 'joke' – and a trio is a subsection, originally, played by three soloists to contrast with the full orchestra in symphonies):

Ex 92

What is even more remarkable than the freshness of the melody is the way in which Schubert's harmony remains faithful to the pentatonic structure of the melody. Bar 3 introduces a B flat in the melody which is extraneous to the basic five-note scale, but Schubert treats this B flat as the basis for another pentatonic structure in a different key. This intuitively right harmonization of pentatonic melody by pentatonic harmony presages by a whole century the theory of modal harmonization of folk music elaborated by Emmanuel, Bartók, Kodály, Vaughan Williams and others. It was no theory with Schubert. In his case it must have been his instinctive melodic gift which made him realize that a folk-type of melody based on a few notes (just as expressive as the speech of simple people can be in a limited vocabulary) needs equally simple harmony which introduces no note foreign to the tune, so that the tune may blossom, as it were, in its own soil.

By contrast, Schubert's music also contains examples of pentatonic melody harmonized chromatically. The following example from the last music he wrote, the Piano Sonata in

B flat (Deutsch 960), has an intensely personal 'accent' in its harmony:

which a few bars later becomes even prophetic of Grieg:

This is unlike anything that was happening in Central European music during Schubert's lifetime, an era ruled by the tyranny of the major/minor scales, relieved only by very occasional reference to the ecclesiastic modes. There is such a wild woodnote in Schubert's B flat Sonata that I personally like to remember that at the time he composed it, he was reading Fenimore Cooper's *The Last of the Mohicans*. The Quintet in C major – another product of that prodigious last year of Schubert's life – is like a documentary in sound of the life of early nineteenth century Vienna. Its opening drawn-out chord, with its long crescendo, is an expression of insufferably pent-up emotion. In this music we meander by the mill streams of Vienna's environs and follow the slightly pompous gait of the bourgeoisie on the city streets; we catch a glimpse of a coffee house scene; we hear the horses hooves on the cobbled court yards of Vienna and we remember Schubert's song, *The Erl-King*; we hear melody as poignant as the smell of honeysuckle and melody that comes in few notes, like last words;

we hear shrouded chorale-chords of death, chords which die like living things into long silence; and we hear the dancing of children, as life goes on. What a work! I once knew a music student who claimed that at University he learned nothing fundamental to life except that one professor said 'Listen to Schubert's Quintet'. And the man who wrote this work – one of the peaks of chamber music – had the humility, in the last weeks of his life, to approach a theoretician, Simon Sechter, for lessons in counterpoint and fugue!

In previous chapters we have seen that great composers sometimes received instruction from other great composers, as in the case of Schütz who apprenticed himself to Gabrieli and Monteverdi. These cross-references are a fascination in music history; but in the case of the Viennese classics, they hardly exist. I say 'hardly', because Beethoven was (nominally) a pupil of Haydn for a short period. But Haydn was no pedagogue and Beethoven was pig-headed. Dissatisfied, Beethoven studied counterpoint with a theoretician, Albrechtsberger, and made a mess of his exercises. In the arts, contrary to bourgeois belief, credentials don't matter. Nothing in the arts can be taught anyway. Everything has to be *learnt*. And doing is learning. One so often hears the question: who was his teacher? – as if teachers are the 'open Sesame'! It is the *spiritual* masters who matter; the affinities that a composer discovers for himself. In this way, Haydn learned from his senior, C. P. E. Bach, and from his junior, Mozart (whom Haydn solemnly declared 'the greatest composer ever'). Heaven knows from whom Mozart learned! Some craft from his father; but he seemed to be born with it and his *juvenilia* – even his *infantilia*! – are mature; almost morbidly so for a youngster. Beethoven, despite his personal disappointment with Haydn, nevertheless learned from his works. And Schubert certainly took Beethoven as a model and guide.

In an attempt to get perspective between the Viennese classics, let us consider what are generally recognized as their greatest works. Haydn's are the two late oratorios, *The Creation* and *The Seasons;* some of the late symphonies (he wrote well over 100) and a few of his piano sonatas. Mozart's greatest works are his last three operas (*Figaro, Giovanni* and *The Magic Flute*), his last three symphonies (he wrote 41), a few of the Piano Concertos and the Requiem. Beethoven's greatest works are Symphonies 3, 5, 7 and 9, Piano Concertos 3–5, the *Waldstein*, *Appassionata* and the last five of the 32 Piano Sonatas; the 'Diabelli' Variations for piano; the opera *Fidelio*; the 'Rasoumovsky' and his late String Quartets; and the *Missa Solennis*. Schubert's greatest works include many of his songs (from the early ones, *Margaret at the Spinning Wheel* – composed at 17 – and the *Erlking*, and, of the last songs, *Die Winterreise* and *Schwanengesänge*); Symphonies 7 ('The Unfinished') and 9; about 4 of his 14 Piano Sonatas (certainly the last two); the String Quartet in G minor, op. 161, and the Quintet, op. 163. If we narrow it down still more, we must say that Haydn's supreme achievement was in choral music, Mozart's in opera, Beethoven's in symphony and piano sonata and Schubert's in song and chamber music. This is a more provocative than definitive judgment. Some would consider Haydn's greatest work to be in his symphonies, but the above list is meant to be *comparative*: that is to say, though Haydn's symphonies may be considered by some as greater than his oratorios, few people would claim his symphonies to be greater than Beethoven's.

A word about the phrase, 'the Viennese Classics'. They weren't classics during their lifetime. Nobody is. A composer *becomes* a classic with time, when his work is seen to be in perspective with a great tradition. But the idea that a great composer is misunderstood during his lifetime is fallacious. A great composer always communicates to some of his contemporaries and has a few detractors; then is appreciated posthumously even more (though a few years after his death there is generally a period when he is forgotten). The word 'classic' or 'classical' implies moderation, proportion, sanity and intellectual control of the passions. In that sense, only Haydn and Mozart are classical; Beethoven is Janus-headed, looking back to classicism and forward to Romanticism; and Schubert is a Romantic whose musicality still almost miraculously allows him to write without immoderation.

Those four composers eclipse their contemporaries, who, even so, included composers of stature. Antonio Salieri (1750–1825) was a Veronese who lived most of his life in service to the Viennese Court. He composed many Italian operas, a handful to German libretti and some liturgical music. He was much sought after as a teacher of Italian word-setting. Beethoven took lessons from him. Salieri was Mozart's rival who did not put in a good word for Mozart when he might. (The legend that Salieri poisoned Mozart is, however, false.)

Beethoven considered the Florentine Cherubini (1760–1842) who became director of the Paris Conservatoire, to be the greatest of his contemporaries. He began by writing liturgical music, became an authority on counterpoint and went on to write operas which combined high seriousness with strong drama, as in his *Medea*, which Callas has done much to reinstate in our own day.

Two other Italians emigrated to England: Muzio Clementi (1752–1832), whose Piano Sonatas were much admired by Beethoven; and Johann Baptist Cramer (1771–1858), Clementi's pupil who is remembered for his piano exercises. Clementi also taught the Irish composer, John Field. Johann Nepomuk Hummel (1778–1837) was a pupil of Mozart and a composer of transparently brilliant piano music and concertos more popular in their day than Beethoven's.

Czechoslovakia was remarkable during this period for producing outstanding composers. Even in the eighteenth century, the English music historian Burney had apostrophised Prague as 'the conservatoire of Europe'. Frantisek Xaver Dušek (1731–99) was a pianist and composer of amiable piano music. His namesake, Jan Ladislav Dušek (1761–1812) was a more considerable composer and, in collaboration with Czerny, the pioneer of the harp/piano duo. He was much travelled, a favourite of Catherine the Great and Marie Antoinette and a friend of Haydn and Spohr. It was this Dušek who first placed the piano sideways to his audience: some said to produce a better sound; others, to display his profile and fingerwork. It was in the garden music-shed in Dušek's villa just outside Prague that Mozart completed *Don Giovanni;* the two were bosom companions and Mozart always spoke with affection about Prague. Antonin Reicha (1770–1836) was a colleague of Beethoven when they both, as young men, played in the Electoral Orchestra at Bonn. Later, Reicha emigrated to Paris and became the teacher of Berlioz, Liszt, Gounod and Franck. He composed for all media, and particularly well for woodwind. His set of 36 Fugues for piano (dedicated to Haydn) contain innovations in rhythm and/or tonality: no. 20 of the set being in five-beat rhythm, which, Reicha's footnote informs us, was characteristic of lower Rhine folk-dances. Vaclav Jan Tomášek (1774–1850) was another serious-minded Czech composer. His corpus includes Goethe-Leider (he was a friend of Goethe). He also strove towards the creation of Czech national music, especially in his setting of the patriotic epos by Karl Egon Ebert entitled *Vlasta* ('Native Land'), which anticipates Smetana's symphonic poem *Ma Vlast*. Tomášek wrote an opera, *Seraphina*, but his piano *Eclogues* and *Dithrambics* contain music of more originality. Jan Vaslav Voříšek (1791–1825) was a friend of Beethoven and Schubert in Vienna. His *Impromptus* for piano influenced Schubert's pieces of the same title.

These composers bridged the period of the Viennese Classics and the new age of Romanticism.

13 Revolution, Romanticism, Nationalism and Realism

For centuries, behind the foreground of cultivated, professional music-making, there was a background of another kind of music: that of peasants, labourers. Their protest against feudalism was voiced in song as well as in speech and action. But these songs of protest sounded in the distance, as if lost in forest depths. The peasants of the English Peasant Revolt of 1381 sang *The Cutty Wren*. As the song was seditious, its words were couched in terms of an allegorical bestiary; but the peasants well knew its meaning:

Every revolution and protest movement has had its songs, but these and other songs of the people only began to impinge upon the European musical scene about the time of the French Revolution or in the Age of Enlightenment which led up to it. Men of action and scholars alike contributed to the incipient interest in folk-lore. Captain Cook's journals of 1769, published in Hawkesworth's *Voyages* (1773) contain the earliest source material on Polynesian (specifically Maori) music, which Percy Grainger, hearing in the first decade of the 20th century, described as the most beautiful folk music he had ever heard (and he had heard more varied folk music than most) – yet this remains, even now, some of the least known. In the years when Cook was voyaging the globe, Thomas Percy, later Bishop of Dromore in Ireland, was domestic chaplain to the Duke and Duchess of Northumberland and busy on his *Reliques of Ancient English Poetry* (1765), a repository of folk lore. In Germany, about the same time, Johann Gottfried Herder, philosopher and philologist, was compiling and translating his *Stimmen der Völker in Liedern* (Voices of the Peoples in Song, 1778/9). Two late 18th century poets who preserved the folk song of their respective countries were Robert Burns the Scot and Carl Michael Bellman the Swede, who was also a composer of popular songs.

When the tidal wave of the American Revolution, the War of Independence (1775–83) crashed on the shores of Western Europe and found echo in the French Revolution of 1789, the voice of the people began to be audible in European music.

On the night of 5th–6th October 1789, the Parisians, marching to Versailles, sang *Ça Ira*, one of the French Revolution's 'theme songs'. Tradition has it that General La Fayette, who had fought in the American Revolution and now was active in the French Revolution, suggested the words of the song to a Parisian street-singer called Ladré. The refrain incorporated Benjamin Franklin's favourite saying from the American Revolution: 'That's the thing!' Ladré's words ran:

> Ah, that's the thing, that's the thing, that's the thing!
> The people on this day will shout without ceasing
> Ah, that's the thing, that's the thing, that's the thing!
> Despite the blacklegs we'll win the day.
> Ah, that's the thing, etc.
> The aristocrats in the barrow,
> Ah, that's the thing, etc.
> The aristocrats to the gallows.

After words like that, the tune was a bit of a come-down. And it needed no little adaptation. Originally it was a theatre dance, *Le Carillon National*, composed by one Bécourt, a violinist at the Theatre des Beaujolais:

La Marseillaise, a tune whose fame makes its quotation unnecessary, was composed by Rouget de Lisle, a French captain of engineers. He composed both words and tune whilst quartered in Strasbourg, during the night of 24th–25th April 1792, in response to the Mayor of Strasbourg's speech which regretted the lack of a rousing song for the volunteers of the Lower Rhine. Next day de Lisle had it scored for military band. A singer named Mireur sang it at a civic banquet in Marseilles to such effect that it was printed and distributed to the Marseilles volunteers who, to its strains stormed the Tuileries (the Royal Palace) in Paris on 10th August 1792. It is inspiriting to realize that what is possibly the (musically) finest national anthem in the world (most national anthems being blown-up bathos) was the work of an amateur musician and poet who was an engineer and soldier. But it is something of an anti-climax to realize that the composer of this splendid republican hymn was a member of the constitutional party and refused to take the oath to the constitution abolishing the crown. Because of this he was stripped of his military rank and imprisoned, to escape only after the fall of Robespierre in 1794. Later he received a small pension granted by Louis XVIII and continued under Louis Philippe. The career of Rouget de Lisle has been dwelt upon a little because it is symbolic and symptomatic of the course of the French Revolution itself, which, beginning with such hopes for the emancipation of the labourers, ended with the entrenchment of the bourgeoisie.

This entrenchment of the bourgeoisie produced a whole crop of middle-class composers of talent, active in the first half of the 19th century. Though some of them incidentally created something of worth, their work as a whole extols the comfortable virtues of *Biedermeier* cosy elegance, prettiness, sentimentality and, *en masse*, is a kind of ode to the *status quo*. Of their number are Bishop with his *Home Sweet Home*, Bishop who was Professor of Music at the University of Edinburgh and later at Oxford; Auber, the writer of titillating *opera comique*; Hérold, the composer of the coyly pastoral ballet *La Fille mal gardé*; Czerny, the indefatigable purveyor of piano exercises for the daughters of the middle-class; Spohr, the German sentimentalist with symphonic aspirations who poured out *pots-pourris* for his instrument, the violin; Lortzing, whose opera *Czar und Zimmermann* ('King and Butler') was full of *gemütlich* tunes guaranteed to raise no eyebrows; the Dane Gade whose attempts to pioneer Scandinavian music were frustrated by his allegiance to Leipzig conservatism; Sterndale Bennett, the English emulator of Mendelssohn and the composer of an *Ode for the Opening of the International Exhibition of 1862* (text by Lord Tennyson) and the Cambridge *Installation Ode* of the same year (text by Kingsley). This is not to say that here and there these talented men did not produce an unusual work. The Swedish symphonist Berwald, while he contributed nothing to the corpus of songs in which Scandinavia was beginning to find its voice through the musical setting of its indigenous languages, nevertheless composed a *Sinfonie Singulière* which is an original piece of music. I am not dismissing minor masters out of hand. The world would be poorer without them. I am simply trying to get historical perspective. All the same, the number of lesser composers in the first half of the 19th century was legion. Even Mendelssohn, a composer of genius, has all the characteristics of bourgeois culture in his rather complacent sense of well-being. And the type of bourgeois composer, whose music gave pleasure but never gave anything to *think* about, was also found, perhaps not quite in such preponderance, in the latter half of the century – as in the cases of the Frenchmen Delibes, who wrote charming ballets, and Massenet, who wrote melodious operas. And their compatriot Saint-Saëns, almost a latter-day Mendelssohn, through his longevity carried the 19th century bourgeois cultural tradition into the second decade of the present century.

The French Revolution and the Enlightenment that led up to it engendered a cultural dichotomy, which can be summed up in the awakening of progressive forces and in reaction to those forces. Sometimes in 19th century music (and for that matter, even in some 20th century music) progressive and reactionary ideas are even co-existent in one composition. The forces of progress looked to the future, were optimistic, humanistic, humorous. The forces of reaction looked to the past and were pessimistic, 'supernatural' and humourless.

We have already dealt with the influence of the French Enlightenment and the French Revolution on French music in what has been said of Rousseau and Gossec. The German Enlighteners, headed by Herder, launched the *Sturm und Drang* ('Storm and Stress') period of German culture at the end of the 18th century. This had an initial progressive impetus. Beethoven's *Appassionata* Sonata of 1804 is an example *par excellence* of this mode of expression. But after Germany had participated in the French Revolutionary Wars and, with other countries, had pursued a policy of opposition and containment of the new forces in France, the German cultural scene became more and more reactionary. A residue of the *Sturm und Drang* expression still lurked in the daemonic energy of Weber's and Marchner's cult of the supernatural in opera; but there was another, more subtle, element in these works. When a bourgeois German opera-goer of the 1820's lit his cigar and relished his glass of hock between the acts of Weber's *Die Freischütz* (1821) or Marschner's *Der Vampyr* (1828), an ingredient of his enjoyment was the ability to be thrilled by fear of the supernatural theatrical spectacle he had been witnessing, but, after it all, to luxuriate in the sense of wellbeing he prized in his everyday life. There was a direct parallel here to the relationship between the German bourgeoisie's narrow escape from the French Reign of Terror. So the German stage, for a generation or so, was filled with monsters and fairies in an age which more and more strove to grapple with problems of actuality.

This cult of the supernatural in opera persisted and was exported from Germany. The Russian, Anton Rubinstein's *The Demon* of 1875 is a late example. But as the century wore on, it became more characteristic to laugh at the foibles of bourgeois life than to seek refuge from reality in the thrills of the 'horror'-opera. In the second half of the 19th century

Offenbach in France, Gilbert and Sullivan in England and Johann Strauss the Younger in Austria all shot darts at bourgeois society in operettas scintillant with tuneful wit.

The 'dark satanic mills' of the Industrial Revolution were the womb of technology, which spawned a new kind of diablerie – that of the human devil performing instrumental wonders. The Italian violinist/composer, Paganini (1784–1840) inspired the Hungarian pianist Liszt (1811–86) to achieve Paganinesque wizardry on the piano. And the French conductor/composer, Berlioz (1803–69) 'played on the orchestra' with virtuosity that matched Paganini's and Liszt's. Just as Liszt 'Paganinized' the piano, the French Jewish composer Alkan (1813–88), an orchestrator *manqué*, 'Berliozized' the piano in writing Symphonies for it. The expertise demanded in the mastery of the modern grand pianoforte and of the modern orchestra was directly related to the technology which developed instrument-building to a high degree of efficiency.

If all nineenth century music had to be destroyed, with the exception of one composer, much of it would still survive in the innumerable piano transcriptions of Liszt. Liszt's development was remarkable. His last works shed all his earlier display and, in their economy and visionary harmony, are often prophetic of the 20th century.

Romanticism was engendered by the cultural ethos of the French Revolution. In the 20th century the word 'Romantic' has been used most frequently in a pejorative sense. But there were actually two kinds of Romanticism: that which represented progress and that which represented reaction. Progress meant struggle for human rights. Heroes died in this struggle. Lord Byron's death in 1824 at Missolonghi, while aiding the Liberal side in the Greek War of Independence, was a romantic symbol that inflamed the imagination of Greek peasant patriots. There was nothing bogus about it. It happened. It was real *and* romantic. Romanticism, in this sense, is that part of reality which is larger, more heroic, than everyday reality; but it is a part of reality all the same. This kind of Romanticism could also be a previsioning of future reality. And it was no less romantic and heroic when workers used their weapon of the strike and faced death in military opposition. These anonyms were every bit as heroic and romantic as Lord Byron, if you accept the reality and cut the legend of the poet's glamourized love-life. Liszt paid tribute to the heroism of ordinary people in his piano piece *Lyon*, which, inspired by the rising of the silk-weavers of Lyon in 1834, bears the motto: 'Living work, or fighting die'.

The piano was the Romantic instrument *par excellence*. It still is. Art is Romantic when it suggests a reality larger than itself. That is why the piano is *the* Romantic instrument; for it suggests the orchestra. It is the only instrument that can.

Eighteen-hundred-and-forty-eight was the year of Europe's revolt, the year of the Communist Manifesto. In that year Liszt composed an *Arbeiterchor* (Workers' Chorus) and in 1849 Schumann composed four Revolutionary Marches for piano, op. 76.

The following year a warrant for Wagner's arrest as a 'politically dangerous person' was issued from Dresden. Liszt, Wagner's friend, procured a passport and escorted him as far as Eisenach *en route* to exile in Paris.

In this age the tempo of events accelerated. Everything was in motion in the world of ideas. Even that most aristocratic and most artificial art, ballet, reflected change. If we review some landmarks in the history of ballet, we see that even this art of kings was becoming transformed:

1734: Mlle. Salle discards the *de rigeur* piled head-dress (*Pygmalion*, London).

c. 1740: Mlle. Camargo wears tights to facilitate the *entrechat a quatre* (crossing of feet in mid-air).

1760: Noverre, *maître de ballet* at Stuttgart, publishes *Lettres sur la Danse* – Rousseauesque ideas of a return to nature and simplification of costume and choreography.

c. 1770: Mlle. Heinel introduces the *pirouette*, a step impossible in the Louis Quartorze style of dancing.

1772: Pierre Gardel discards the mask.

1827: Mlle. Taglioni's Paris debut. The greatest name in ballet. The skirt is raised above the ankle to display the limbs. She uses flexible sandals with stiffened toe-cap for dancing *sur les pointes*.

The meaning of music in the Romantic era became more specific. Ideas in music were revealed as much as – more than! – Taglioni's ankle.

Romantic music was often 'programmatic', that is, it was suggested by an idea from literature, painting, sculpture, nature, personal or historical events. Sometimes, as with Berlioz, these so-called extra-musical ideas were the *point d'appui* for a work. (For my own part, I doubt if any idea with emotive 'overtones' *can* be extra-musical.) At other times, as with Schumann, the title was added after composition of the music, as an aid to the listener to appreciate the composer's intentions.

Schumann's fanciful titles most often related to the world of children. As Cyril Scott once wrote perceptively about Schumann, 'With him true romance was associated with childhood, not with maturity.' Schumann (1810–56) was the son of a Saxon bookseller. His romanticism was nurtured by browsing through his father's books and later by his passion for the novels of Jean Paul Richter and E. T. A. Hoffmann. Schumann was a pianist *manqué* who maimed his right hand by practising piano exercises with a home-made contraption for supporting his weak fourth finger, which suffered from writer's cramp. He married his piano teacher's daughter, Clara Wieck (who was 9 years younger), only after litigation. Theirs was a true marriage, such as few artists experience, comparable perhaps only to that of Robert and Elizabeth Browning. In 1840, the year of Schumann's marriage, he composed some 200 songs in a burst of joy. Previously he had written only short piano pieces. Clara was one of the outstanding pianists of her age and also a composer in her own right. She performed her husband's works all over Europe and in Russia. Schumann ordered his creative life with admirable German thoroughness, devoting separate periods to concentration on orchestral music, chamber music, then choral works. He was also active as a music critic and founder and, from its second year, editor of the *Neue Zeitschrift für Musik* (established 1834). He championed new music from Chopin to Brahms. He wrote about an imaginary society, the *Davidsbündler* (the 'Companions of David') who waged war on philistinism. Schumann was aware of a dichotomy in his nature: the dreamer and the man of action. The first he called Eusebius; the second, Florestan. He signed articles by these names. The dichotomy of the whole Romantic era – advance into the future, retreat into the past;

progress and reaction – was symbolized by Schumann's dual nature. Tragically, he became schizophrenic, attempted to drown himself and spent his last years in a mental home. Clara Schumann (1819–96) was a heroine who lived in memory of her husband and to support their children. She was befriended by Schumann's protégé, Brahms (1833–97).

Schumann was profoundly interested in the psychology of women and of children. These interests are his most progressive aspects. Examples are his song cycle *Frauenliebe und-Leben* (A Woman's Love and Life) and his collections of piano pieces, *Album for the Young* and *Scenes from Childhood*. In addition to the educational importance of his music, he showed understanding of woman in an age which abused women. The 19th century produced no woman composer comparable in genius and passion with the novelist and poet Emily Brontë. But the existence of Emily Brontë and, in ancient times, of Sappho, and in recent times, of Isadora Duncan, indicates that women can contribute to culture just as significantly as men have done. The reason why they have not done so in such numbers as men certainly relates to the way in which the structure of society has militated against women. Schumann contributed to the emancipation of women through the depth and sensitivity of his understanding. In the 20th century, women are beginning to take their place in musical life. Though centuries of subjection to second-rate citizenship cannot be overcome overnight, the great women composers will surely appear.

Whereas Mendelssohn (1809–47) was content to emulate the Beethoven of the 'Pastoral' Symphony by writing such generalized programmatic works as the 'Italian' and 'Scottish' Symphonies, and, at the same time, realized that his lesser gift required compression of material, Schumann and Brahms were bolder in emulation of Beethoven. Schumann must have been struck by the transition to the *finale* of Beethoven's 5th Symphony – that passage which sounds like coming out of a tunnel into daylight, symbolizing lust for liberty. Though Schumann knew his gift to be less than Beethoven's, he identified himself with this music and its message of freedom and emulated it worthily in the transition to the finale of his own 4th Symphony. Brahms must have admired these passages in Beethoven and Schumann for he wrote a transition to the *finale* of his 1st Symphony which clearly belongs to their lineage. But whereas Schumann was active in the years that led up to the Revolution of 1848 and alive to the atmosphere of the age, Brahms composed in the aftermath of the failure of that Revolution and his work vacillates between an impassioned pessimism and a sense of complacent well-being. Brahms also reacted against programmatic music.

Some schools of criticism have taken a superior, patronizing view of programmatic music, deeming it more 'intellectual', more 'respectable' to profess admiration for so-called 'absolute' music. (As if anything made by man can be absolute!) In fairness to the Romantics, despite their occasional abuse of programmatic detail in music (for it is not music's function to represent in detail), in historical perspective, it seems that their use of fanciful titles to describe their compositions may have been motivated by an awakening awareness that they were trying to write a music of ideas. Bidding farewell to an age when music was the toy of aristocracy, they were beginning to realize that music was a higher form of speech and to speak without meaning was an insult to intelligent listeners. Besides, there were burning issues of the day and music which merely made pleasing and ingenious patterns was not the music for the age of advancing humanity. Even some of the classicists, Bach and Couperin among others, had written music with fanciful titles. But, for a time, the theories of the anti-Wagnerite Hanslick seemed to present a clever argument against even the possibility of a music of ideas. His essay *Vom Musikalisch Schönen* (Of Musical Aesthetics, 1854) conceived music as fundamentally a play of beautiful sounds, like some sonal fountain. This overlooks the fact that music is a moving language in both senses – it moves and has emotion; whereas the fountain plays without any emotional impetus. All the same, Hanslick was a musically cultured critic who was also an excellent pianist and amateur composer. He did not deny music's power of expression: he only doubted that this expression could be specific. Unfortunately, his theories were perpetuated by critics lacking his culture who reduced his ideas to desiccation.

The marathon opera – sometimes extended to five acts – was a feature of the first half of the 19th century in the work of composers based in Paris, such as the Italian Spontini the Frenchmen Berlioz and Halévy, and the Germano-Frenchman Meyerbeer. For their subjects they went to the past: Berlioz to ancient Troy in *Les Troyens*, Meyerbeer to the Middle Ages in *Les Huguenots*. This aggrandizement of the past had a broadly reactionary basis, coming in the aftermath of the French Revolution, though here and there were indications of contradictory progressive ideas, even within the context of reaction.

But contemporaneously with these gargantuan works, other composers were writing in miniature forms. Whereas the composers of the epic spectacle-opera tended to be cosmopolitan in their orientation, the miniaturists were beginning to grapple with a new idea that was dawning on the European horizon: the idea of nationalism. Herder had been the first to theorize about nationalism in the arts, but the Irish composer Field (1782–1837) and the Pole Chopin (1810–49) didn't theorize about it: they wrote nationalistically because they were exile sons of down-trodden tragic nations. Field was the first Celtic voice in cultivated European music. Field's melody often grew out of the ethos of Irish or Scottish folk song. The opening tune of his *Nocturne Pastorale* for piano is almost identical to the *Skye Boat Song*:

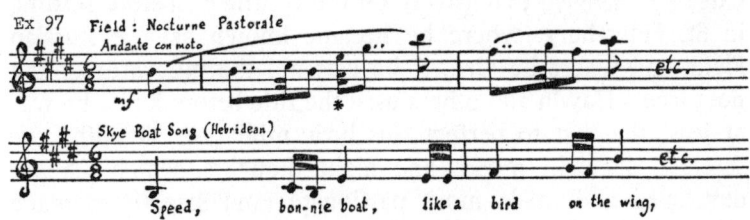

The 'Scots snap' rhythmic figure (indicated by an asterisk in the above example) crops up in a number of Field's other compositions, while the slow movement of his first piano Concerto in E flat consists of variations on the Scottish folk song *Within a Mile of Edinburgh Toun*. Another element in his melody was the Irish drawing-room ballad which the poet Tom Moore popularized in his *Irish Melodies*, the six volumes of which were published in Dublin between 1807 and 1834. Moore wasn't the first to cultivate the drawing-room ballad: Field, brought up in Dublin, would assuredly hear earlier examples. (And of course, this ballad tradition – a kind of cognate bourgeois art form distantly related to folk song – extended into the 20th century in the repertoire of the Irish tenor John McCormack and in the Scottish 'Songs of the Hebrides' collections of Marjorie Kennedy-Fraser.) Another element in Field's melody was *fioriture* ('flowered') embellishment. This was a pianistic treatment of the embellishments which early 19th century opera singers were wont to add to the melodies of Bellini and other composers of *bel canto* opera. (*Bel canto* signifies the perfected art of pure singing, that is, the fusion of mastery of vocal production with the purest lyric tone.) An innovation in Field's piano writing was his characteristic use of wide-spread *arpeggio* figures ('harped' chords, that is, one note played after the other as on a harp) sustained in a cloud of pedal-held sound. This technique of *arpeggio* accompaniment was a pianistic treatment of the music of the Irish harpers, notably the celebrated blind bard, Turlogh O'Carolan, whose son published a collection of his father's music and, like Field, left Dublin for London. As an adolescent, Field demonstrated pianos in Clementi's London warehouse. Later he travelled extensively on the continent, before settling in St. Petersburg, where he became known as 'the Russian Field' and where he died. If he was not the innovator of the nocturne – Haydn and others used the title before him – he was at least the first to perfect this lyric miniature, distilling the serenity of night moods and night thoughts, which Chopin developed and made more passionate (and sometimes made almost oriental in its mysterious voluptuousness.) Like Field, Chopin, apart from a very few chamber works, wrote exclusively for piano solo or for piano and orchestra (though Chopin's orchestration was rudimentary).

On November 2nd 1830 the twenty-year-old Chopin left Warsaw for ever, to pursue a career in Paris. With him he took a casket of Polish earth. After a brief but glorious career he died in Paris on October 17th 1849. The Polish earth was cast on to his coffin on 30th October at the funeral in the Pere-Lachaise Cemetery in Paris, where so many musicians and artists (among them, Rossini, Cherubini and Oscar Wilde) are buried. On March 1st 1879 the urn containing Chopin's heart was sealed in a pillar of the Church of the Holy Cross at Warsaw. Physically, Chopin was a consumptive; his taste was aristocratic; but his spirit was heroic and revolutionary. And, above all, he was a Pole. His patriotism found voice in his Polonaises and Mazurkas. His Polonaises are music of soldiers; his Mazurkas, music of peasants. It is in his Mazurkas that we hear the strange melodic intonations which are the direct counterpart of peasant dialect-accent:

But Chopin also absorbed in his music something from France, his seat of exile; and his father, though living in Poland, was born in France. This French aspect of Chopin pervades his Valses.

Chopin's Impromptu in F sharp, op. 36, contains more aspects of his style than any other single short piece he wrote. It begins with a French-like (almost Poulenc-like!) pastoral melody:

contrasting with its second section, which is cast in the heroic Polish mould:

Later in the piece a 2-bar transition reveals Chopin's enquiring mind in music that, out of context, might easily be taken as mid-20th century in style:

and the final section is an example of the salon-like embellished piano writing that Chopin developed from Field.

In terms of nationalistic significance, Chopin's most important works are the Mazurkas. But three sets of his other works are important for other reasons: the Preludes, Studies and Ballades. The 24 Preludes are epigrammatic utterances, sometimes (as in no. 2) of strikingly 'modern' harmony. The 24 Studies are perfect examples of exploration of various facets of piano technique (each Study isolating one particular technical aspect) wedded to a sense of poetry unmatched by any other composer of piano studies, with the exception of Liszt, who perhaps achieves this degree of perfection in only one of his studies, *La Leggerezza*. And Chopin's 4 Ballades are his most successful foray into large-scale form – more successful than the two Piano Sonatas, though the *finale* of each of the Sonatas is remarkable: the B flat minor for its dissonant monody, the B minor for its indomitable rhythm. Chopin's Ballades embody his heroic aspirations. Tradition has it that in composing them, he had in mind certain programmatic suggestions from the ballad poems of his fellow countryman and contemporary, Adam Mickiewicz, some of whose poems he set to music in his small corpus of 17 songs. In his book *The Rising of the Polish Nation in 1830 and 1831*, published in Paris in 1834, Maurycy Mochnacki (who, besides being an active revolutionary, participant in and historian of the Revolution of 1830, was also a virtuoso pianist and Chopin's friend) wrote: '... at that time all that was poetic was patriotic. And so literature in Poland, like the people, began to conspire. Adam Mickiewicz, was (although perhaps he did not know it) as great a politician in his poetry as Lelewel was a great poet in his politics, that is, in history and historical criticsm.' Chopin, as is well-known, loved George Sand (Madame Amandine Lucile Aurore Dudevant), that cigar-smoking, trouser-clad semitic beauty who was also a militant feminist and socialist, as well as being the most prolific authoress in literature. She and Chopin met in 1836 and their attachment lasted till 1847. The usual interpretation of their relationship – namely, that George Sand was maternal to her 'petit Chopin' – is inadequate because it concentrates on psychological aspects to the neglect of their communion of thought on the revolutionary content of their work.

Cultural nationalism did not flourish in those countries which had achieved autonomy and/or which were conscious of their cultural heritage, as France, Germany and Italy were. It was found in countries under the yoke of another, more powerful country. Such oppressed countries were Ireland, Poland and Czechoslovakia. Nationalism also found expression in Russia, which was oppressed from within by its Czardom, so that its greater masses were suffering serfdom at a time when the masses of most of the rest of Europe were becoming conscious of the potential power of proletarian unity. In France, Germany and Italy, musicians were brought up in the great cities where no folk song was sung, but in countries such as Czechoslovakia and Russia, musicians were more often brought up in the provinces and the country where there was much folk song to be heard. These factors influenced the growth of national music.

Liszt was the father figure of the rise of nationalism in 19th century music. He encouraged every school of nationalist composers. His experiences as an emigré Hungarian who became a great cosmopolitan, probably whetted his appreciation of the vividness of national colour and character in music. His own attempts at writing 'Hungarian' music was not a true development of the folk ethos but a glamourization of gypsy music which was not specifically Hungarian but was also found in the Balkan Peninsula, Rumania and Transylvania.

Smetana was present in Liszt's circle at Weimar in 1857 when the Viennese conductor-composer von Herbeck declared that, though Bohemian fiddlers were legion, not one Czech composition had contributed significantly to European music. This statement (which wasn't entirely true) goaded Smetana into creating a national style in Czech music. The emergence of Czech music cannot be understood properly without awareness of the nation's struggle for independence. Czechoslovakia did not exist until 1918, that is, until the collapse of the Austro-Hungarian monarchy. Yet the Czechs have upheld their language from time immemorial. In ancient Czech the word *jazyk* denotes both 'nation' and 'language'. After the overthrow of Bohemian independence in 1620, the use of Czech declined. Under the Austrian suzerain, there was wholesale burning of books in Czech, and, being banned from schools, it became almost extinct. Dobravsky, who died in 1829, was the pioneer for the revival of Czech, yet even he doubted that it could again be widely known, which it was by the mid-19th century. Smetana (1824-84) grew up during this period of cultural revival and extended it to the field of music. His path was beset with problems. At 24 he wrote a letter, a *cri de coeur*, to Liszt, confiding that his existence was one of semi-starvation and begging a loan of money. He added that even in his 17th year he 'knew neither C sharp nor D flat'. Liszt replied, not with money but by arranging for the publication of Smetana's opus 1, a set of piano pieces. Further difficulties were heaped on Smetana by his support of the abortive revolution of 1848, in connection with which he composed a March for the Student Legion. The failure of the revolution bred rancour and squabbling among Czech patriots. When a conductor's post was offered in Sweden, he seized it. Distance brought perspective to his patriotism and deepened his convictions. When he returned to Prague in 1859, his hour was ripe. Italy's victories over Austria relaxed the iron grip Austria had wielded over the Czechs. Indigenous culture began to burgeon. No Czech contributed more to its full flowering than Smetana. Tragically, towards the end he suffered the maladies of both Beehoven and Schumann: he became both deaf and mad.

Whereas Smetana, the brilliant pianist, emulated Liszt, Dvořák (1841–1904), emulated Brahms. Whereas Smetana achieved his greatest work in opera (notably *The Bartered Bride*) and the cycle of six symphonic poems (*Má Vlast*), Dvořák achieved his in the symphony (notably *From the New World* and the 7th in D minor, op. 70). Dvořák's melody is richly inflected – inflections that relate to the dialect-accent of the composer whose first job was as a butcher's assistant and who, however far he travelled, remained true to his origins.

And nationalism began to emerge in the North. Richard Nordraak (1842–66) inspired Norwegian nationalism in Edvard Grieg (1843–1907). Himself a composer of songs fragrant with Nordic folk-idioms, Nordraak's early death kept his memory ever-young for Grieg, for whom Nordraak became a symbol and challenge. Grieg's student years were spent in Leipzig, but Teutonic academicism ran off his back. He was tiny in person; with his snow-cloud of hair and gentian eyes he seemed to be the offspring of Puck and a troll. His natural delicacy of health was latterly impaired by the loss of the functioning of one of his lungs. This restricted his daily composing time to two hours and so prevented the creation of extended works. But Grieg had a Viking heart. His finest music is still almost entirely unknown. For all its miniature dimension, like himself it too has a Viking heart. His *Den Bergtekne* ('Taken into the Mountains') for baritone, two horns and string orchestra, is a setting of an old Norwegian folk text about a lad who got lost in the mountains, carried off by the troll's daughter (symbol of the giant forces of nature). Writing to the dedicatee of this work, Grieg expressed himself with characteristic pungency: 'I knew yours was one of those frightful natures that demand blood; and a nature like yours will not look long before finding spots and stains here and there of sheer heart's blood. But who has the feeling for such things?' This element is less apparent in his celebrated Piano Concerto and in his *Peer Gynt* music though it is here too. Among Grieg's many pretty album-leaves for piano, this same strength is also sometimes felt, particularly in his Norwegian Folk Songs, op. 66 and in the *Slaater* (Peasant Dances), op. 72, which, composed in 1906, might even be mistaken, in certain highly dissonant passages, for the music of Bartók. His solo songs, written for his wife, Nina, are certainly some of the most passionate in song literature, particularly the heart-wrung, *I love thee*. Grieg's last work, the Norwegian Psalms, op. 74 for *a capella* choir, is also amazing: one of them is even bi-tonal (in two keys at once) and here the rich, almost Wagnerian harmonic language is applied to choral writing of consummate skill with an expression of wounding poignancy which cries out from the north wind and is as sharp as icicles. Debussy's well-known quip about Grieg – 'a pink *bon-bon* stuffed with snow' – is as glib as it is unfair, and shows he could not have known Grieg's finest music. Besides, Grieg exercised a subtle influence on the French Impressionists, as Ravel freely acknowledged, and also on the English Post-Impressionist, Delius.

Nationalism in Italian music emerged only in the second half of the 19th century. At the beginning of the century, the shadow of Napoleon was cast over Italy and, after the Congress of Vienna (1815), the country was under Austrian suzerainty. It was only in 1861 that Italy became a unified nation. That sequence of historical events is paralleled in the operas of Rossini (1792–1868), Donizetti (1797–1848) and Verdi (1813–1901). Rossini took operatic subjects from French literature: *The Barber of Seville*, based on Beaumarchais, *Semiramide* based on Voltaire, and his last opera *William Tell* was written to a French libretto and cast in the French grand manner of the Meyerbeerian five-act opera, though it was later re-arranged in four acts. Rossini settled in France and almost totally abandoned composing after his 37th year. Donizetti's opera *Daughter of the Regiment* concerns the love of a Tyrolean peasant for the 'daughter' of the French Grenadiers who turns out to be the daughter of a Marquise. Of course, both Rossini and Donizetti abound in Italian gaiety and grace – the benison of growing up with sunshine and wine – Rossini having perhaps more gaiety, Donizetti maybe a little more grace – but it is not till we come to Verdi that we begin to sense that here is music from a compatriot of such Italian revolutionary nationalists as Garibaldi and Mazzini. Verdi's opera *The Masked Ball*, scheduled for premiere in Naples in 1858, was banned by the censorship because of its inflammatory content. Verdi refused to revise the work to conform with the censor's requirements, and this stand received much publicity and made him a national hero. His name was chalked on Italian city walls and associated with the initials of the patriotic slogan 'Vittorio Emmanuele Re d'Italia' (Victor Emmanuel King of Italy).

Let us pursue the comparison of Rossini, Donizetti and Verdi a little further. Rossini wrote consummately for voices; he himself was a trained singer. There is something Olympian about him which his humorous laziness prevented from attaining full grandeur. (Beethoven wrote four overtures for one opera; Rossini made one overture serve four operas!) Donizetti is a transitional figure between Rossini and Verdi. If Donizetti had written less – he wrote about 70 operas as against Rossini's 50 – he might have achieved more. Even so, he wrote what is probably the most superb ensemble number in Italian opera, the sextet from *Lucia di Lammermoor*, which is as full of grace as it is of psychological delineation of the six characters; and it served as a model for Verdi's quartet from *Rigoletto*. But neither Rossini nor Donizetti evince the span of development shown in Verdi's long career. In this respect, perhaps only Beethoven is comparable to Verdi. From Verdi's first opera, *Oberto, Count of Saint Boniface* (1839) to his last, *Falstaff* (1893), there is traced a trajectory of development amazing in its range. His first operas have rudimentary accompaniments, platitudinous recitatives, mediocre orchestration and their weak sense of form is redeemed only by the spark of melody; but his last operas get away from the sectionalized form of set arias by adopting Wagner's idea of 'through composition' (that is, the unfoldment of the drama in a constant flow of music) without sacrificing the element of song; their orchestration teems in masterstrokes; and the accompanimental figures throb with vitality and reflect dramatic psychology with uncanny insight. Verdi was fortunate in his librettist, Boito (1842–1918), who was also an opera composer in his own right, his best known opera being *Mefistofele*.

Verdi, apart from opera, created one of the finest musical monuments in the 19th century ecclesiastic music in his *Requiem* of 1874, which is like a paean to the divinity in man himself. It is totally free from the cowering masochism and sentimentality which sometimes characterized 19th century ecclesiastic music. Only two other 19th century ecclesiastic works are comparable to Verdi's *Requiem*: the German *Requiem* of Brahms (1867), which is a sober, dignified and sometimes touching tribute to the moral spirit of Protestantism; and Berlioz's *Requiem* (1837) which, with its panoply of four brass bands, each placed in a corner of the concert hall or cathedral, plus a large orchestra, choir and soloists, is pagan rather than Christian and is a colossal study in the macabre; reminiscent of Victor Hugo's characterization of the Western arts as 'the apotheosis of the grotesque and the sublime', as distinct from the serene, static and ecstatic Nirvana of the Oriental arts.

In the 1860's a huge seismographic disturbance was registered in the tribulations of the human spirit: the American Civil War. It too had its folk songs of protest, such things as *Marching through Georgia*. Since the Puritan crew of the 'Mayflower' had landed in New England in 1620, the pioneers of the New World had been too busy surviving and killing Red Indians, and too busy building roads and towns, then railroads, to have time to cultivate much music in the Central European sense. But one folk minstrel of the Burns or Bellman type emerged: Stephen Foster (1826–64), a poet and composer of songs that have been sung in every country in the world – such as *Old Folks at Home*, *My Old Kentucky Home*, *Beautiful Dreamer* and nearly 200 more. He was a 'wild-flower' composer whose spontaneous lyricism needed academic training no more than a fine natural folk-singer needs it. He came from Irish stock and some of his melodies have a Celtic turn of phrase. Though born in Pittsburgh, Pennsylvania, he identified himself with the negroes of the South, in much the same way that Joel Chandler Harris did in his *Uncle Remus* tales. Present-day Afro-Americans perhaps criticize Foster's paternal attitude to the negro, but historical perspective must allow him an important place in American song. And when the Civil War came, he wrote songs in the cause of the North – such as *We are coming, Father Abraham, 300,000 More*. America was in revolutionary ferment during the 1860's. An indication of just how high this revolutionism ran is contained in the true anecdote that, when the Russian Czar heard that an American revolutionary delegation was visiting the Great Exhibition at the Crystal Palace, London, in 1851, he forbade the Russian delegation to attend! Times change.

The second half of the century witnessed what was certainly the most powerfully nationalistic school of composers of the whole century: the Russians. Their spokesman, the critic Stasov, called them the *kuchka*, or the 'mighty handful' or the 'mighty five'. Their leader was Balakirev (1836–1910). He was a virtuoso pianist and expert score-reader (that is, he was able to take a full score, containing music for the full orchestra, and play a 'digest' of it on the piano) and so he was able to perform, interpret and criticize the works of other members of the group. They held critical sessions at which Balakirev was 'in the chair'. This was necessary, as they were all amateurs and needed direction: Borodin (1834–87) was a research chemist; Cui (1835–1918) and Mussorgsky (1835–81) were military men; and Rimsky-Korsakov (1844–1908) was a naval officer. Balakirev took Glinka (1803–57) and Dargomizhsky (1813–69) as the father figures of Russian nationalism. They too were dilettantes. Glinka had a few piano lessons from John Field, but it was folk music that acted as a catalyst to his creative gift. He travelled much – Poland, France, Spain – and everywhere it was folk music that attracted him. His outstanding achievements were the large-scale operas *A Life for the Czar* and *Russlan and Ludmilla*. Glinka's style was lyrical, whereas Dargomizhsky's was declamatory. Dargomizhsky's work culminated in the opera *The Stone Guest (Don Juan)* of 1872, after Pushkin. Borodin and Cui were essentially lyrical composers and Balakirev and Rimsky shared a predilection for exoticism and semi-orientalism; Balakirev in his *Islamey* fantasy for piano and his symphonic poem *Tamara*, Rimsky in his opera *The Golden Cockerel*. Mussorgsky's outstanding works were the opera *Boris Godunov* and the suite for piano, *Pictures from an Exhibition*. Mussorgsky was a great realist in music. He realized the autochthonic peasant nature of the Russian masses, half-starving, illiterate, dressed in rags, yet with latent revolution smouldering within them. Mussorgsky was an alcoholic and left much of his work unfinished. Rimsky-Korsakov, who was a master of orchestration (on which subject he wrote a text-book which is comparable with the similar textbooks of Berlioz, Strauss and Widor), took it upon himself to try and complete Mussorgsky's works. In the process he re-orchestrated them and sometimes emasculated their harmonies. These revisions, however well-intentioned, revealed a lack of affinity between the composer and his reviser. There have been later revisions of Mussorgsky's work – particularly by Shostakovich – which have enabled more of the original to come through.

Contemporaries of the *kuchka* who were more oriented to Western Europe, though still Russian for all that, were Tchaikovsky (1840–93) and Anton Rubinstein (1830–94). Tchaikovsky was perhaps the greatest of all composers of ballet music and he is at his most Russian in this. 'Balletomania' is inseparable from love of his music for *Swan Lake* and *The Sleeping Beauty*. And Tchaikovsky brought a balletic element into everything he wrote. Even his 6th Symphony, the *Pathétique* has a lovely second subject – one of the great melodies – which in its poise recalls a *tableau* in a ballet; and the second movement of this symphony, a dance with 5 beats per bar, is an example of how he revitalized symphonic form through 'cross fertilizing' it with balletic forms. The symphony is a large enough form to be all-inclusive. In Berlioz's *Fantastic Symphony*, subtitled *Episode in an Artist's Life*, the symphony becomes the repository for an essentially theatrical mode of expression. From this detailed programmatic Berliozian symphony, Liszt went on to conceive the idea of the symphonic poem, a single movement work of a detailed programmatic nature, also containing symphonic development. Another source of Liszt's symphonic poem was his transcription for piano and orchestra of Schubert's 'Wanderer' Fantasy, which gave him the idea of metamorphosis of themes.

Anton Rubinstein is one of those figures generally overlooked in histories of music, one of those who are sure to be the butt of supercilious comment, though his Promethean piano-playing gained universal acclaim. His innovation of the biblical opera had neither success nor successor. Much of his vast output is undeserving of exhumation, but there are among his songs – particularly the highly original *Persian Love Lyrics*, one of which Chaliapin recorded in a superb rendering – and his piano music (particularly the startlingly modern 6th Barcarolle), works which deserve to be performed.

But the cataclysm in 19th century music was the German Wagner (1813–83). It is difficult for us to imagine the impact he had on his contemporaries. The well-known caricature of Wagner splitting the listener's ear-drum with hammer and chisel is one small indication of his assault on comfortable sensibilities. The sheer volume of sound he desired was overpowering. Berlioz too had unleashed orchestral thunderbolts, but Wagner's were mixed with more potent fire and brimstone because he used orchestral 'doublings' more than Berlioz did: that is, Wagner concentrated huge forces of different instruments playing the same note – a more lavish, more 'poster' style of sound-painting than Berlioz's, which was characterized by a more fastidious Latin intelligence and a masterful knowledge of the capabilities of each instrument employed (which a detailed analysis of Wagner's scores reveals that he did not possess to the same degree).

Wagner was born in Leipzig and, when he was only six months old, his father died. His mother soon remarried. Her second husband was a celebrated actor, Ludwig Geyer. So the infancy of the future master of music drama was played out against a backdrop of real-life theatre. He scribbled plays before he attempted to compose. In his adolescence Wagner studied in Leipzig. He travelled a good deal, to Vienna and Prague. Already the wanderlust was there. Then at 20 he was a chorus master in Würzburg. In the same year, his first complete opera, *The Fairies*, Weber-inspired, was produced in Leipzig. Within a few years he held a succession of minor Kapellmeister posts in various small German towns. At 23 he married an actress, Minna Planer. The next year he had a post in Riga (Baltic Russia). The year after that he visited London and Paris and met Meyerbeer, whose monumentalism and huge popularity he emulated in the 5-act opera *Rienzi* (1842). In that year, he is back in the city of his childhood, Dresden, as

Kapellmeister. In the *Flying Dutchman* (1843) Wagner epitomizes his own restless spirit. But just as his wanderings brought him back every time to Germany, his attempts to ignite revolution in art ended by retreat into the past. His earlier operas deal with legends of medieval chivalry (*Tannhaüser, Lohengrin*) or the medieval guilds (*Mastersingers*); and even in this earlier period he begins to go further back in history, to Celtic and Nordic mythology, to *Tristan and Isolde*, until, in his last period, he takes as his subject the myths of the Rhine in *The Ring*. As a kind of coda *in excelsis* to his career, he goes back to the medieval 'Holy Grail' legend for his final opera, *Parsifal* (1882). The earlier operas contain symbolic flashes of Wagner the political revolutionary, as when Rienzi leads the insurrection of the Roman people against the nobles; or, again, when Tannhaüser defies the tame moral code of the minnesingers and bursts out with a sensuous hymn to Venus; or, again, when Lohengrin refuses the title of Duke, preferring to be styled Protector of Brabante. But the theme is generally the not very revolutionary one of sinful man's redemption through prayerful woman. From *Tristan*, that is from 1860, pessimism begins to stain Wagner's music a Plutonian purple. The *Mastersingers* is one last flash of colour, humour and humanity before this monumental career becomes engulfed in the mists of Rhinish legends and lost in the incense of *Parsifal*. Wagner made his own private life public and through his many loves and the desertion of his first wife for Liszt's daughter Cosima (who was first married to the Liszt pupil von Bülow), Wagner seemed to retrace the experiences of his own mother – who knows whether to find the father he never knew? In terms of his art, this meant a tortuous trek after the ideological father-figure concept of pure Aryan Germanness. This concept was fodder to Hitler's Third Reich. There were even elements of incipient Nazism in Wagner's pompous and bulky literary works: his essay *Art and Revolution* was oriented to Nazism rather than Marxism, and his essay on *Jewishness in Music* has an anti-semitic bias. The libretti which Wagner wrote for his own operas are of slender literary value in contrast to their bulk. But Wagner's opera reforms extended the line of Monteverdi and Gluck: herein lay his real importance. Opera wasn't enough for him: it had to be *music drama*.

The orchestra wasn't enough: he had to have 'Wagner tubas' built to plumb deeper depths of orchestral sound. He dispensed with the stylistic artifice of recitative and set aria. In their place he put his ideal of 'unending melody'. He heightened the role of the orchestra: a Wagner plot unfolds in the orchestra even more than in the voices. As 'sign-posts' to the direction of the drama, he coined the idea of the *Leitmotif*, or 'leading motive', that is, a melodic fragment associated with a particular dramatic character. Sometimes this technique clarifies the drama; at other times it has an obvious effect analogous to the display of placards. The *Leitmotif* is related to Liszt's 'metamorphosis of themes', which he employed in his symphonic poems and to Berlioz's *idée fixe* (the use of a symbolic recurrent musical phrase in different contexts) employed in the *Symphonie Fantastique*.

Wagner was both fortunate and unfortunate in his patron, the mad King Ludwig II of Bavaria, through whose assistance (and through public subscription) he was enabled to have his own opera house at Bayreuth, which was opened in 1876. Fortunate, because of the opportunities this offered. Unfortunate, because Bayreuth was the sarcophagus of Wagner the revolutionary. Perhaps Wagner channelled his old revolutionary fervour into planning and supervising the building of the opera house of his dreams, which was built with superb acoustics and with an enclosed orchestral pit to effect blend of timbre.

The opening of the famous *Tristan Prelude* stands as a symbol of the whole of Wagner. It's 'love-death wish' aspires with revolutionary ardour, only to fall away in disillusion:

Harmonically, Wagner's post-Tristan music is like a desert of shifting sands. It reflects multi-coloured mirages. But the future could not build on it. Wagner was the fallen colossus in the desert.

F

Culturally, Wagner's music epitomizes the peak of 19th century capitalism, before it lapsed into the crack-up of imperialism; a culture luxuriating in grandeur and splendour but oblivious to squalor and poverty; a world of ideas populated by gods and godesses instead of men and women, and unblessed by children. Bernard Shaw's 'perfect Wagnerite' interpretation of *The Ring* as a gigantic socialist symbology refers, rather tortuously, to the text rather than the music. But all that this interpretation boils down to is a generalized conclusion that lust for power brings disaster. Lust for power – disaster: that is another description, in stronger terms, of the opening of the *Tristan Prelude*. Wagner's music certainly lusts after power in climax after climax, and these successive climaxes ultimately pall into disillusion. Wagner the Romantic retreated from revolution into a manhandling of mythology; his nationalism was bloated jingoism; and he lacked realism. Like the Bismark helmet, Wagner's music had a phallus on top of it instead of a brain inside it. Wagner's friend and enemy, the philosopher Nietzsche, was perhaps his only contemporary who understood the nemesis of the Wagner problem.

Wagner was certainly one of the largest figures in the history of music: perhaps only the Beethoven of the Ninth Symphony or the *Missa Solennis* has the same kind of largeness. It is therefore all the more disappointing to realize that Wagner's mighty genius, which was once addressed to the cause of humanity's struggle, ended by being displayed in a personality-cult festival with superb acoustics, marvellous staging, top-rank artists – and astronomic prices; a festival which Karl Marx described as 'a stupid celebration in honour of a court musician.'

In the tail of the great comet that was Wagner, there were a host of luminaries sparked off. There was Humperdinck (1854–1921), the composer of the Wagnerian opera for the kindergarten, *Hansel and Gretel* (1893). Though he lived into the present century, he is included here because he belonged to the Wagnerian aftermath. A more considerable figure who also belonged to it was the *Lieder*-composer Hugo Wolf (1860–1903), who applied the psychological commentary of Wagner's orchestral accompaniments to the piano accompaniments of songs. Indeed with Wolf the piano is much more than accompaniment. Another figure who emerges from out of Wagner's shadow is Anton Bruckner (1824–96) whose symphonies seem to be inspired by that vastly prolonged time-scale of the sustained chord of E flat major which opens Wagner's *Ring*, the symbol of the majestically flowing Rhine. But the statement often made that Bruckner is Wagnerian music drama applied to the symphony, is incorrect. For a symphony can not rely, as opera does, on tracing the development of a literary text; it must be concerned more with architectonics. Bruckner became aware of this as he laboured at his nine symphonies (1868–94). Whereas Wagner was the Protestant revolutionary who retreated into medieval legends, Bruckner was a medieval type of simple devout Catholic who happened to be born in the 19th century, the century of revolution, and who prepared the way for later epic symphonists, such as his pupil Mahler and, much later, Shostakovich. Bruckner also wrote much ecclesiastic music.

César Franck (1822–90) was in some ways a Franco-Belgian counterpart of the Austrian Bruckner. He also was a pious man of a retiring nature, revered by his few intimates, and otherwise almost unknown during his lifetime. Unlike Bruckner, he only wrote one Symphony, written, like all his other best works, late in his career; but this Symphony and his Violin and Piano Sonata evince outstanding melodic quality in every theme. The Symphony also embodies the innovation of 'cyclic form', that is, a thematic cross-reference between movements. This idea was developed from the symphonies of Schumann (and there is even a hint of it in Beethoven's Fifth). Franck was also a distinctive harmonist whose chromatic progressions are highly personal, memorable and recognizable. (It is a tribute to the variety of human thought that the later composer Delius, using harmonic means almost identical to Franck's, nevertheless also sounds entirely *sui generis*.) Franck represented a reaction against the opulent world of French grand opera. He wrote no opera but confined himself to orchestral, chamber, choral and organ music. He was organist at Saint Clotilde, Paris. Liszt admired his organ-playing.

Public taste in the second half of the 19th century found the Meyerbeerian opera too grandiloquent. The operas of

Gounod (1818–93), *Marguerite* (later exaggeratedly re-named *Faust*) and his *Romeo and Juliet*, were graceful, tuneful works with nothing Goethean or Shakespearean about them.

Just as Gounod reacted against Meyerbeer, Bizet reacted against Gounod. Gounod had cut down the size of opera but had made it more 'perfumed' and sentimental. Now Bizet (1838–75) cut out the sentimentality and replaced it with realism. A sharp Gallic realism. Its apogee is the opera *Carmen* (1875), which many different types of musicians have admired and which is certainly one of the most perfect operas. One should not confuse Bizet's realism with naturalism. Naturalism in any art over-emphasizes physiological aspects. Examples of it are the novels of Zola, Bizet's contemporary and compatriot; and yet Zola's theory of the novel ran counter to his practice, as may be seen in his *Le Roman expérimental* (1880) and *Le Naturalisme au théâtre* (1881). Bizet's realism – unlike the *verismo* school of Italian opera (Leoncavallo and Mascagni) – does not concentrate on the physiological but accepts it and penetrates to the psychological. The set for the first act of *Carmen* is a square in Seville with a cigarette factory. The music is not foreign to the scene. Meyerbeerian music for this scene would be ridiculously grandiose; Gounod would have reduced the factory to a huge chocolate box through his saccharinity. Bizet is neither grandiose nor saccharine. He is essential. And that essentiality has both life's bitterness and sweetness. It shrinks neither from a musical response to Carmen's body nor to her untamed spirit. Bizet wrote other operas and orchestral and piano music – he was a brilliant pianist – but *Carmen* is his masterpiece.

One of *Carmen*'s first admirers, Chabrier (1841–94) also left a marvellous evocation of Spain interpreted by a Frenchman, in his orchestral rhapsody *España*. This has a frank acceptance of the physical with an intensely communicated sense of the enjoyment of life, of the smells of fruit-stalls, the relish of gay colours and conviviality. Chabrier, visiting Seville in 1882, wrote a letter to some friends of his which shows how realism of the *Carmen*-type had emancipated music from its courtly past: 'Eh bien! mes enfants – What an eyeful we're getting of Andalusian behinds wiggling like frolicsome snakes! Every night finds us at the *bailos flamencos* (*sic*), surrounded both of us by *toreros* in lounge suits, black felt hats cleft down the middle, jackets nipped in at the waist and tight trousers revealing sinewy legs and finely modelled thighs. And all around the gipsy women singing their *malaguenos* or dancing the tango, and the manzanilla circulating from hand to hand that everyone is forced to drink.'

14 The Twentieth Century

Ours is an age of contradiction: famine in the East while the West destroys surplus produce; the age in which the U.S.A., the leading capitalist country, does not make a decisive victory over Vietnam, one of the smallest nations. At the beginning of this book, there is a statement about art reflecting reality. This is borne out by the chaos of music in the twentieth century. Because the music scene is so complex, there is no point in devoting an inordinately long chapter to it. That would only add perplexity to complexity. Besides, we are too near to our age to see it in focus and perspective. So this chapter will be as brief as the subject will permit.

There are some dozen different schools of music in the twentieth century. I list them in a rough chronological order, approximately the order in which they became generally known.

1. French Impressionism.
2. German Expressionism.
3. Cosmopolitan neo-classicism.
4. American Jazz.
5. Neo-nationalism.
6. Gebrauchsmusik ('utility' music).
7. Soviet socialist realism.
8. Cosmopolitan dodecaphony.
9. Serialism.
10. Electronic music.
11. Aleatoric ('random') music.
12. 'Folk' and 'pop'.

French Impressionism and German Expressionism are fag-ends of reactionary Romanticism, though they seemed new in their day. Nineteenth century Romanticism in music was often inspired by literary sources. Impressionist and Expressionist music were inspired by painting. Debussy (1862–1918) was the outstanding French Impressionist composer. He was influenced by such late-19th-century Impressionist artists as Manet, Monet and Renoir. Ravel (1875–1937) is also sometimes referred to as a French Impressionist composer, though he was less intuitive, though more elegant, than Debussy. Two English Impressionists were Delius (1862–1934) and Cyril Scott (1879–1971). Debussy was a great admirer of Cyril Scott. The Austrian Jew, Schoenberg (1874–1951) was the outstanding Expressionist composer. He was not only influenced by the great Gustav Mahler (1860–1911), whose symphonies and songs bridge Romanticism and Expressionism, but also by such German Expressionist artists as Kandinsky and Kokoschka. Schoenberg was a painter himself and, with those Expressionists, was a member of the *Blaue Reiter* ('Blue Rider') group of artists about the time of the First World War. Debussy and Schoenberg both dealt with the subject of Maeterlinck's fairy tale of doomed love *Pelléas et Melisande;* Debussy in a dream-like (at moments, nightmare-like) opera (1902), Schoenberg in an intense symphonic poem (1903); each composed without knowledge of the other. French Impressionism engendered music of gourmet-like selection: music of intentionally restricted means which, with few strokes, as it were, painted a hazy, luminous picture in sound, often with a descriptive title. It sometimes employed the whole-tone scale, a scale of six notes containing no semitones but only tones (for instance, the notes C, D, E, F sharp, G sharp, A sharp), which produced atmospheric, 'cloud effects' in sound. Impressionism sought to capture, as in a musical snapshot, some fleeting glimpse of the outer world of landscapes, sea-scapes, street scenes. Expressionism, on the other hand, did not content itself with fleeting glimpses of an external world but with an interior world of psychological studies in sound. It employed all twelve notes of the octave in dissonant combinations which sought to break free from the old law of gravity-in-sound called tonality. This music – for example, Schoenberg's Piano Pieces op. 11 (composed in 1908)

– came to be described as 'atonal', a designation, however, which Schoenberg himself disapproved. This dissonant, free use of all twelve notes with few or no recognizable sound-patterns, but with a flowing themelessness, produced an effect of intense introspection and brooding subjectivity. Impressionism was hedonistic: music of the enjoyment of life. Expressionism was 'problematic': music which tells us that life is earnest. Impressionism could be bizarre and whimsical, as in some of Debussy's Preludes and even more in the miniatures of the Scoto-French Erik Satie (1866–1925). Expressionism, on the contrary, had little or no humour but could be grotesque, as in Schoenberg's *Pierrot Lunaire* (1912) for speaker and five instrumentalists.

The orchestral and piano music of the Russian Scriabin (1872–1915) lies somewhere between Impressionism, and Expressionism. Whereas Chopin influenced his early works, a study of Theosophy influenced his later compositions, in such works as his third and last Symphony (*The Divine Poem*), *The Poem of Ecstasy* and the *Poem of Fire* for orchestra, piano, organ, choir and colour keyboard, which 'translated' the music into colours projected on to a screen during the performance, in accordance with Scriabin's colour theory of music (the idea that each note or key corresponded to a different colour of the spectrum). Scriabin devised a scale on which much of his later music is based; like the Impressionistic whole-tone scale, with which it has five notes in common, it is a six-note scale, comprising C, D, E, F sharp, A, B flat. From this scale Scriabin derived what he called a 'mystic' chord; like the characteristic chord-structures of Schoenberg, it is built in superimposed fourths:

Ex 103

Though Scriabin was a friend of the Marxist Plekhanov and though his music sometimes was inflamed by revolutionary-like fervour, his hierophantic works bore an indirect rather than

THE TWENTIETH CENTURY

direct relationship to what was happening to the great masses in Russia at the time. In these mystic works, Scriabin turned his face away from such scenes as Maxim Gorky showed in his play *The Lower Depths* (1902) and, instead, sought to write a music of the individual human soul, outside the context of society, much as Elgar had done in his oratorio *The Dream of Gerontius* (1900).

Though a new age stirred in the Russian Revolution of 1905, many composers seemed oblivious to it. The Russian Stravinsky (1882–1971) wrote his *Firebird* Suite in 1910, a brilliant score whose orchestration dazzles like Imperial jewels. The German Richard Strauss (1864–1949) wrote symphonic poems on medieval subjects (*Till Eulenspiegel, Don Juan,* etc.) and operas based on ancient mythology (*Salome, Elektra*) or on the vulgar glory of the parvenu Vienna of Maria Teresa (*Rosenkavalier*). All these works contain delights, but they fail to plumb depths because they reflect, not so much a world view of the beginning of the 20th century (a world view such as Beethoven's at the beginning of the 19th) but only the relatively comfortable side of life that these composers – Scriabin, Stravinsky, Strauss and others – knew.

One escape was to compose pastiche 'in the old style'. The German Max Reger (1873–1916) did this. Consummate contrapuntal skill, invention in chromatic progressions and mastery of variation form sometimes made his music sound like a development from Brahms, especially the *Variations and Fugue on a theme of Bach* for piano.

The Italian composer/pianist, Busoni (1866–1924) was a champion both of classical music, particularly Bach and Mozart, and of new music. In Berlin between 1902 and 1909, he organized, conducted and financed (at a cost of £25,000) a series of Berlin Philharmonic orchestral concerts in which music by the then unknown Bartók, Debussy, Delius, Elgar, D'Indy, Nielsen and Schoenberg was premièred. Busoni's piano transcriptions from Bach are well-known; less well-known is his transcription of Schoenberg's Piano Piece op. 11, no. 2 (1909).

In 1905 Busoni wrote the longest and grandest Piano Concerto of all, a work that lasts for 75 minutes and calls for a male chorus to extend the range of sonority in the finale. His *Fantasia Contrappuntistica*, which exists in five versions for different media (1910–22), is a monumental and visionary completion of the unfinished fugue from Bach's *Art of Fugue*. Busoni wrote four operas, the last of which, *Doktor Faust*, is a 20th century masterwork. He was a philosophical eclectic. He thought about music and its relationship to life, science and philosophy. As a young man, he gave street corner orations on Marxism to German workers in Leipzig. He had an outstanding literary gift as well as being a musical genius. He was a fine essayist and aphorist. His later music is an attempt to create what he himself called a 'new classicality', which he defined as 'the mastery, selection and use of all durable results of previous experience and experiment and their embodiment in firm and beautiful forms'. He was a neo-Renaissance figure who, during his lifetime, was overshadowed by his contemporary and compatriot Puccini (1858–1924), a lesser though powerful and more immediately popular composer of *verisma* opera.

During the First World War, Stravinsky sent a question to Busoni, conveyed through a third person: 'Why are you, a well-known champion of the new, such an admirer of the classics?' Busoni replied that, if Stravinsky also knew the classics, he too, would admire them. The next thing that happened was that Stravinsky, the aggressive modernist, wrote *Pulcinella*, a ballet based on themes by the 18th century Italian classicist Pergolesi. And in 1924 Stravinsky wrote his so-called 'back-to-Bach' Piano Sonata. This period of Stravinsky's career is called the neo-classical style. In the Twenties and Thirties, Stravinsky lived in Paris and his neo-classicism influenced *Les Six*, the French group of composers (Auric, Durey, Honneger, Milhaud, Poulenc and Germaine Tailleferre) who had the playwright Jean Cocteau as their spokesman. But neo-classicism was a self-conscious striking of attitudes and adaptation of cliches, an escapist Arcady a thousand miles removed from Busoni's concept of new classicality.

Stravinsky, *Les Six* and the English conductor/composer Constant Lambert also toyed with jazz, but a study of the history of jazz makes their toying seem very superficial; for jazz is a peoples' music, the music of the American negro, a race more despised and rejected than even the Jews, and long denied the weapon of education which the Jews have had to combat their adversaries. The African legacy in jazz is not its rhythm, for African rhythm is much more complex, but its melodic ululation, the 'blue' note (a note sung off pitch, slightly flat), the sliding attack and the hiccough-like acquittal of a phrase. Perhaps jazz rhythm evolved through the need for these melodic features to break free from the restricting hymnal harmonizations imposed on negro slaves by white Christian evangelists. Syncopation – off-beat rhythm – certainly tried to break loose from the regular beats of music notated by bar-lines. Jazz refused to be music behind bars – in both senses. In this off-beat rhythm was the Afro-American's dream of liberty. From such embryogenesis jazz was spawned in Storyville, the French Quarter of New Orleans, Louisiana, known as 'The District' or 'Tenderloin', the only district in the States where prostitution was tolerated by law. There was even a published directory of 'The District' called *The Blue Book*. But jazz was a part of everyday negro life, not only part of its night life. It grew from brass band playing on street parades and funeral processions and from bands riding through town on trucks to advertise a dance. Buddy Bolden's was the first jazz band. They played in Storyville in the early 1890's. The personnel included cornet, clarinet, trombone, banjo or guitar, double bass and drums. The early bands had grandiose names, such as The Imperial Band or The Original Superior Orchestra. Mississippi steamboats took jazz up the great river and its tributaries. St Louis was one of the main stops en route. An all-white band, called The Original Dixieland Jazz Band, who had absorbed their music in New Orleans, were the first to make New York aware of jazz and the first to make jazz recordings: that was in 1917. They added a piano to the Bolden-type ensemble. In 1917, on U.S. Navy Department orders, Storyville closed down. Jazz moved up the Mississippi to Chicago. Sacked Storyville workers got new jobs in Chicago stockyards and steel mills. Prohibition in the Twenties made the Windy City the main port for bootleggers and bred a flourishing underground night life. King Oliver's Creole Jazz Band was the first to score a 'hit' in Chicago. Louis Armstrong played in this band, under Joe Oliver's lead. Chicago phonograph companies began to record jazz. It began to be played in big dance halls and the bands were augmented to fill a more spacious acoustic. Now that it began to be played to white audiences, it became smoother and more sophisticated. It also began to be written down and played from sheet music, instead of improvised as it had been from its inception. Smart sets of white Americans culted it. Scott Fitzgerald's Jazz Age was in full swing, though 'swing' itself came later – diluted jazz. (Read Scott Fitzgerald's essay 'The Jazz Age'.) Jazz was another fashion for the bored rich. Some negro jazzmen, to the credit of their bank balance and the debit of their soul, entertained white folks in nightclub versions of an Uncle Tom or Jim Crow act. The word 'syncopation' was bandied about and appeared frequently in band names: Peyton's Symphonic Syncopators, Power's Harmony Syncopators, and so on. The names sounded good. The jazz itself didn't. The pulse of jazz grew weaker as the trumpets blared louder. Soft white audiences liked the baby-voiced 'wow-wow' mute which strangled the voice of jazz when it threatened to become too obstreperous. Jazz was whitewashed.

But in the decline, there was still a galaxy of jazz stars. 'Jelly Roll' Morton and his Hot Peppers; Art Tatum; Louis Armstrong; 'Fats' Waller; and Duke Ellington. Morton claimed to have 'created jazz' around 1901 – a foolish claim. He took it to court, challenging W. C. Handy who composed and published the classic *St. Louis Blues* in 1910. Morton lost his case and became a broken man. He was an elegant jazz pianist who loved to make free transcriptions from the classics. The blind Art Tatum also did that. He was the most phenomenally virtuosic of all jazz pianists. Rakhmaninov and Horowitz used to go along to U.S. night clubs just to hear Tatum play. Rakhmaninov declared that, if Tatum had been classically trained, he could have been comparable with any pianist in the world. 'Fats' Waller was a more happy-go-lucky pianist, a kind of more rotund version of the eccentric Chopin specialist, De Pachmann; both Waller and De Pachmann interlarded their playing with verbal comments. Armstrong died in 1971, but Ellington is still with us. Armstrong (or 'Satchmo' – 'Satchel Mouth') was *the* great jazz trumpeter. Ellington is an innovator: he was the first jazzman to notate group improvisations and to make them the basis for compositions; he extended jazz forms from the 12-bar blues, the Charleston, the cakewalk and the rag, to the form of the jazz suite, sometimes transcribed from the classics; and he brought the negro spiritual into jazz. The finesse of his sonorities is remarkable, as is his fastidious pianism, the melodic freedom of his slow, controlled *glissandi* and the conversational character of his polyphony. 'Trad' became 'mod' after the second World War. This was largely a 'white' influence. It masked jazz. The ex-cowboy pianist Dave Brubeck was one of the leading exponents of 'mod' jazz. Some negro jazzmen – notably the 'cool' trumpeter, Miles Davis – adopted these sophistications and refined them behind an anti-mask. Others went on playing Uncle Tom. In the 1950's American composer Gunther Schuller coined the term 'third stream', meaning music containing both jazz and classical elements, to differentiate it from 'trad' and 'mod'. 'Third stream' has been developed by the American Bernstein, the Hungaro-British Seiber, the Englishman Dankworth and the Australian Don Banks. Their music is a more sophisticated development from what Gershwin (in his negro opera *Porgy and Bess*) and Weill (in his *Threepenny Opera*) were doing between the two World Wars.

Though jazz is mostly instrumental music, an important body of it is the vocal blues. This has a classic form, comprising 12 bars. The first line of the poem is repeated as the second; this afforded the blues singer time to invent the words of the third line which 'capped' the verse, as the blues was originally improvised. Often the words carried biblical allusions and were full of the philosophy of the underdog. Bessie Smith and Ella Fitzgerald were the outstanding blues singers.

It is symptomatic of white subjection of negroes that no negro composer was recognized till about 1900, when the London-born Samuel Coleridge-Taylor (1875–1912), son of a Sierra Leone doctor of medicine and an English mother, began to gain fame. He was an R.C.M. student of the Irishman Stanford, who was friendly to him but who constricted his fine lyric gift by stereotyped academicism. Coleridge-Taylor's music has a distinctive melodic voice. His *Hiawatha* Trilogy (1898–1900) enjoyed a great vogue with British choral societies until World War II. His *Elëanore* is one of the great love-songs of all time, worthy to stand beside the finest of Schumann and Grieg. Coleridge-Taylor never forgot his African

origin and paid tribute to it repeatedly, most notably in his
5 Choral Ballads, op. 54 and his 24 Negro Melodies for piano,
op. 59.

The first American negro to receive a bachelor of music
degree was the Canadian-born composer/pianist, Nathaniel Dett
(born 1882). The American folk musicologist, Natalie Curtis
(1875–1921) described Dett's chorus *Music in the Mine* (dedicated to Percy Grainger) as embodying that side of negro life
which depicts 'the strong light-hearted labourer who sings at
his work'.

African and American negro music made a powerful statement for the cause of national art. Nationalism continued to
develop in other countries struggling under subjection. Jean
Sibelius (1865–1956) voiced Finland in seven great symphonies;
Finland, where patriotism laboured long under the Czarist
yoke. Sibelius's compatriot Yrö Kilpinen (1892–1959) voiced
Finland in 700 songs, a remarkable testament for humanity
in an age of anti-humanity and mechanization. Kilpinen
is the greatest *Lieder* composer of the 20th century.

The customary view of nationalism in music is that it was
a phenomenon of the 19th century and was exploded by the
first World War. But closer investigation reveals that nationalism was a 'hardy annual' that kept growing into our own age.
Indeed, it is a political truism that nationalism is even more a
phenomenon of the 20th than of the 19th century, as more
nations have achieved independence in our age than ever
before. If the 19th century was a period of cultural nationalism, the 20th is an era of neo-nationalism.

Ignace Jan Paderewski (1860–1941) Polish patriot, pianist
and composer, was the first musician to become a Prime
Minister. At the Versailles Peace Treaty of 1919, he signed
the charter of Poland's independence. Superficial musicians
only remember Paderewski's little Minuet in G, a drawing-room favourite of yesteryear. But Paderewski's *oeuvre* contains
considerable works, notably his monumental 'Polish' Symphony
in B minor, his big Variations and Fugue op. 23 (which contains
some remarkable harmony and is one of the finest piano works
of the 20th century) and his 3-act gypsy opera, *Manru*.

Karol Szymanowski (1882–1937) is the greatest Polish
composer since Chopin. After falling under the successive

influences of Scriabin, Richard Strauss and Stravinsky, in his final period he became interested in developing symphonically the folk music of the Polish Alps. His Mazurkas for piano are examples of this, as is his *Symphonie Concertante* for piano and orchestra. He wrote in all forms. His 3rd Symphony, subtitled 'Song of the Night', is an example of Szymanowski's interest in the orient. It is scored for orchestra, chorus and tenor solo. The poem is from the Divan of Jallaluddin Rumi, the great Iranian poet.

The Russians Glazunov (1865–1936) and Rakhmaninov (1873–1943) carried the 19th century Russian national school into our own age. Both wrote symphonies which have recently been reappraised. Glazunov was an inheritor of Rimsky-Korsakov's brilliantly exotic orchestration, while Rakhmaninov's predilection was for more sombre orchestration, as in his symphonic poem *Isle of the Dead*. Rakhmaninov was one of the most creative pianists ever. In the finale of his recording of the Chopin B flat minor Sonata (the so-called 'wind over the graves') he moulds the music like clay: the result is a unique sound, spectral and diabolic, a vision achieved through mastery of fingering and pedalling. This *diablerie* also characterized his performances of his Piano Concertos.

A concomitant of nationalism was folksong collecting. Outstanding among field-work collectors were the Frenchman, Louis Bourgault-Ducoudray (1840–1910); the Dane, Evald Tang Kristensen (1843–1929); the Englishman Cecil Sharp (1859–1924); the Hungarians Bela Bartók (1881–1945) and Zoltan Kodály (1882–1962); and the Australian Percy Grainger (1882–1961).

The Dane Carl Nielsen (1865–1931) born on the Isle of Funen, like Hans Andersen before him, paid tribute to his birthplace in his cantata *Springtime on Funen* (1921). With Thomas Laub, Nielsen edited a songbook for Danish schools. His six Symphonies bear comparison with the seven of Sibelius. Indeed I would risk the statement that Nielsen's 5th symphony is the finest of the 20th century. It appeared in 1922, the year of Joyce's *Ulysses*. Like that novel – and like that time (the rise of Hitler) – it plays dice with thunderbolts. Its furtive opening is fraught with implicit drama which becomes explicit in bellicose percussion. The hostile mood abates and a broad song opens like a landscape. Rhythms erupt again and a symphonic struggle ensues of such elemental power as to suggest an historic cataclysm. At the climax the score instructs the side drummer to improvise and attempt to quell the music's progress. The destructive force fails to dam the music's current and the first movement ends quietly victorious but exhausted. The energetic second and last movement, with its dialectical fugal writing, is phoenix-like. One of the twelve children of a poor Danish family, Nielsen remained loyal to his background. His music is simple, direct and tough. It is also complex and unflinchingly exploratory. So far, Nielsen is the greatest composer of working-class origin.

Heitor Villa Lobos, the Brazilian (1887–1959), is the most famous composer of Latin America. He is the only celebrated composer to have started as a street musician, a member of the 'choroes' groups of Rio de Janeiro. He was a virtuoso guitarist and cellist and a good pianist. He is one of the most prolific composers of all time. His series of works entitled *Bachianas brasilieras* fuses the spirit of Bach with the content of Brazilian folk music. Villa-Lobos also worked hard as a music educator of the young. The Hungarian Kodály, the Russian Kabalevsky, the German Carl Orff and Villa-Lobos are the four outstanding educationists among 20th century composers.

White American music found its first outstanding name in Edward MacDowell (1861–1908). He followed the 19th century fashion of going to Germany as a kind of musical 'finishing school'. Unfortunately, too often it finished non-German composers in every sense! But MacDowell, a sensitive, susceptible nature, did manage to preserve something of his ancestral Celtic spirit and his American birthright. Indeed, he may be considered as the first American nationalist composer, with an admixture of a personal kind of Impressionism. He has much in common with Grieg and Schumann; like them, excelling in piano miniatures, songs and the piano concerto form. Some of his piano pieces are redolent of America – and he is seldom given credit for this – such things as *From Uncle Remus* and *From an Indian Lodge* (both in *Woodland Sketches*) and *of Br'er Rabbit* (*Fireside Tales*). Like Schumann, MacDowell succumbed to mental illness and died young.

THE TWENTIETH CENTURY

Other composers who fused Impressionism and nationalism were the Spaniards, Albeniz (1860–1909) and Granados (1867–1916), both virtuoso pianists and writers of virtuoso piano music. They also wrote Spanish operas. Granados's *Ballad of Love and Death* from *Goyescas* (impressions of Goya's paintings) is perhaps the finest written-out improvisation in the whole of piano literature. Albeniz's *Triana* is certainly one of the most exciting *tours de force* for piano (and also so unwieldy to play that Leopold Godowsky re-wrote it, improving its pianism immeasurably but not its musical essence.)

Manuel de Falla (1876–1946) carried Spanish nationalism into our own age. His work blends nationalism with neo-classicism. Inspired by Landowska, he wrote a Concerto for harpsichord and incorporated this instrument in his opera *Master Peter's Puppet Show*. His *Nights in the Garden of Spain* for piano and orchestra is a post-Impressionist work, a development from Granados in its glittering colour; but generally his tonal palette favours more austere and sombre hues. His last work was a monumental opera *Atlantidas*.

In chronological order, the next American composer after MacDowell was Charles Ives (1874–1954), though he avoided the limelight and his work only began to be known much later, only through the championing of another American composer, his friend Henry Cowell. In the late 1960's there was something like an Ives vogue. Ives was a director of an American insurance company, a weekend composer, an inspired amateur. He was a primitive, who produced in music a more grandiose 'Grandma Moses' type of art. He was like an aggrandized Erik Satie. His work is a hotch-potch of barn dances, Shaker hymns, military marches and evinces a fascination for experiment. He said he wanted to 'stretch peoples ears'. He experimented with extreme dissonance and irregular rhythms years before Stravinsky and Schoenberg. His music celebrates America. His *Concord* Sonata for piano is a tribute to the New England Transcendentalists, Emerson, Thoreau and the rest. Unfortunately, Ives never thoroughly mastered music notation and his printed works are full of anomalies and ambiguities. In a period such as the present, which cults youth, instant success and sensationalism, these serious shortcomings in his work are considered – if considered at all – not to matter. Naturally, these notational ambiguities multiply in his orchestral works, which need a vast amount of editing.

In my opinion, the most characteristically American composer – the one who sings Walt Whitman's and Carl Sandberg's America *and* is a thorough professional – is Roy Harris (born, appropriately enough in a prairie log cabin on Lincoln's birthday in 1898). Harris came up the hard way and had a number of jobs, including that of a lorry-driver, before he opted for music. His Symphony no. 3 is an American masterpiece.

Aaron Copland (born 1900) is another American who has composed from the American ethos, in such orchestral works as *Appalachian Spring*, *Rodeo* and *Billy the Kid*. Since World War II, however, he has been more interested in assimilating Central European serialist techniques (of which more later). He has also engaged in work with youth and has written cogently about contemporary music.

It may come as a surprise to people who enjoy the traditional national music of Scotland – the fiddle music and the pipe music – to realize that Scotland has so far had only one composer of European stature; and he is still almost unknown – F. G. Scott (1880–1958), the song composer. Single-handed he created a tradition, compound of pibroch, folk-song, ballads (Border, bawdy and drawing room), pub songs and an awareness of Central European techniques. His MacDiarmid settings are his best. No British music from the Twenties is nearer in idiom to middle-period Schoenberg than certain passages in Scott's MacDiarmid songs, in particular, *Country Life* (1923), *Crowdieknowe* (1924) and *Moonstruck* (1927). Scott wrote little, published (at his own expense) only about 100 songs and a small body of choral music. His output is uneven, but the best of it is precious in the best sense. He never did anything to further his cause: a man of dour integrity. Singers who sing German should not fight shy of investigating Scott's settings of Lowland Scots (Lallans) which is phonetically comparable to German.

Relationships between speech and song were investigated by the Czech composer Leos Janáček (1854–1928) perhaps in greater depth than by any other composer. Unlike Bartók,

Janáček never separated analysis of folk melody from its words or its social background. Janáček notated in music many phrases from ordinary everyday Czech conversation and these notations influenced his brusque, ejaculatory thematic invention in his song-cycle *The Diary of One who Disappeared* and his operas, *Jenufa*, *The Excursions of Mr. Broucek*, *Kata Kabanova*, *The Cunning Little Vixen* and *The House of the Dead*.

In Janáček's music, nationalism operates in the most concentrated area of the melodic motif; in the music of the Swiss-American Jew, Ernest Bloch (1880–1959), however, it is racism (naturally, not in its pejorative sense), rather than nationalism, which provides the creative spur and it operates in the most diffuse area of invention – that of rhapsodic form. Bloch's best known example of this is his Rhapsody *Schelomo* for 'cello and orchestra (1915).

I think I have cited enough national composers to make it clear that this school contains a greater number of considerable figures than any other single school of 20th century composers; which bears out my previous remarks about cultural nationalism reflecting the growth of political nationalism in our age. To read some of the younger music critics, one would think that cosmopolitan serialism had become world-wide, whereas it has made little impact on Latin America, Africa or Asia, or on the Western music public at large; and its representatives are known to musicians rather than to music lovers (musicians are not always music lovers!) The 20th century composers who have had a real impact on the concert-going public are almost all nationalists: such names as Bartók, Elgar, Falla, Gershwin, Respighi, Sibelius, Prokofiev, Vaughan Williams, Holst, Shostakovich, Britten and many more.

A militant voice in the cause of women composers was that of Ethel Smyth (1858–1944), who, a daughter of a British General, served a 2-month jail sentence in 1911 as a suffragette. She composed a *March of the Women*. Operas of hers were produced in Germany before the 1914 War, notably *The Wreckers*; and Beecham staged another, *The Boatswain's Mate* in London in 1916.

In the Twenties the German Hindemith (1895–1964) interested himself in *Gebrauchsmusik*, that is, music written for amateurs and dilettantes, to meet some practical need, such as utilizing generally available instruments, perhaps the accordion (very popular in Germany), the guitar, and so on. This movement was a counterpart in music to the functional 'Bauhaus' school of architecture led by Walter Gropius. Hindemith was an immensely practical all-round musician. He began as a virtuoso viola-player but latterly conducted more. He was also a born pedagogue of Teutonic thoroughness who wrote excellent textbooks on harmony and the craft of composition. Near the end of his life, the philosophico-metaphysical strain in his thinking became more evident. His opera *Mathis der Mahler* (Matthew the Painter) was a symbolic protest against Nazism. In the mid-20th century Hindemith has suffered eclipse. If justice is done, he will surely be re-assessed as one of the key figures of 20th century music and one of the few masters in a chaotic era characterized by lack of mastery and even the lack of any wish for mastery.

The subject of Soviet socialist realism is, in a Western world of capitalist propaganda, an ideological battlefield strewn with slogans. Zhdanov (1896–1948), the Soviet Minister of Culture, has even been described in the Western press as 'a lesser Hitler' – to say the least, an emotive expression. What was wrong with the Zhdanov administration was not its fundamentals of aesthetics but the indiscriminate way in which its criticism was meted out. We cannot do better than quote the definition of socialist realism given in *A Dictionary of Philosophy*, edited by Dixon and Saifulin, and published by Progress Publishers, Moscow, 1967. It reads: '*Realism, Socialist*, an artistic method presupposing a truthful, historically concrete reflection of reality taken in its revolutionary development. Its essence is fidelity to the truth of life.' This comes very near to Carl Nielsen's aphorism 'Music is the sound of life'. Engels laid the foundation of Marxist aesthetics with the theory of reflection, which is a basic concept of materialist epistemology and which postulates that the outer world acts on human reflexes and so conditions, positively or negatively, everything that mankind creates. A whole succession of philosophers and art historians have developed the Marxist aesthetic: Chernyshevsky, Plekhanov, Lenin, Gorky, Lunacharsky and Asafaev, among others. Unfortunately, comparatively little of this body of work has been so far translated into English. Before 1933 there were two Unions of Composers in the U.S.S.R.: the Union of Symphonic Composers and the Union of Light Music Composers. In 1933 they amalgamated into the Union of Soviet Composers. In the Twenties, the symphonic composers – Shostakovich among them – had heard 'modernists' works performed in the U.S.S.R.: Berg's opera *Wozzeck*, for instance, and some Hindemith. Some of the Soviet composers emulated these imported works. When the two Unions of Composers amalgamated, light music composers were vociferous in criticizing these 'modernist' tendencies. They were a Union in name but not united in aesthetic. There were stormy meetings, congresses like shouting matches, polemical headlines in *Pravda*. Some of the arguments were crude; some of the conclusions too glib; the optimism didn't always ring true; but Soviet intellectuals and the Soviet State were taking music seriously. They even arrived at a general agreement that the music which would most truthfully reflect the new Soviet State would be nationalist in form and socialist in content. Many years later, even Britain has its Arts Council and its Composers' Guild; but the financial position of most British composers is so precarious that Composers' Guild meetings discuss financial problems rather than music. In the last analysis, it is the *music* and the public's reaction to it that matter. The fact is that the Soviet Union has produced composers who have communicated with the concert-public of the world's five continents: Prokofiev (1891–1953), Myaskovsky (1881–1950), Khachaturian (born 1903), Kabalevsky (born 1904) and Shostakovich (born 1906). In a recent book, Aaron Copland asks why no younger Soviet composer is known in the Western world and assumes that alleged State dictatorship of art has caused ossification of creativeness. I am sure the answer is not as simple as that. A country which was embroiled in revolution only half-a-century ago has understandably felt a need to export only its best artists as representatives of Soviet progress. This happened in the case of the great pianist Sviataslav Richter, whom the Western World did not hear until he was about 40 years of age. And only now is the West becoming aware of composers younger than Shostakovich, such as Sviridov (born 1915) and Shchedrin (born 1932).

From my visits to East Europe, I would say that musicians there are *au fait* with 20th century Western music to a much greater extent than Western musicians are aware of *their* music. Very few Western musicians have heard of such fine composers as Vladigreov, Pipkov and E. H. Meyer, for example. But the so-called 'Soviet block' is not as 'monolithic' as is often made out. Those countries within it which have inherited a Catholic culture – Czechoslovakia, Hungary and Poland, for instance – present a cultural dichotomy. Catholic culture is related to idealist philosophy. Belief in the abstraction of God sometimes exists together with belief in abstract art; that is, an art rooted not in this world but in an 'other' world in which an individual is abstracted from his social context in the contemplation of idealized form without content. Some of Lutoslawski's later music (he was born in Poland in 1913) demonstrates this orientation to sophisticated Western standards in art, though in the music of another Polish composer, Penderecki (born 1928), particularly his *St. Luke Passion*, one can hear a music of human content struggling for expression through a music of abstraction, in which method often plays a bigger part than meaning.

On a summer walk with his pupil Josef Rufer in 1922, Schoenberg declared: 'I have discovered something which will guarantee the supremacy of German music for the next hundred years.' This discovery was dodecaphony. This unwieldy word is a misnomer: intended to refer to the twelve notes of the octave divided into semitones, its etymology actually refers to twelve *voices*. (The word derives from the Greek *dodeka*, meaning 'twelve' and *phone*, meaning 'voice'.) Schoenberg defined dodecaphony as 'composition with twelve notes related only to each other'. Actually, Schoenberg was not the 'discoverer' he imagined himself: the discoverer of dodecaphony was Josef Mathias Hauer (b. 1883).

In Chapter 12 Wagner's post-Tristan harmony was described as 'like a desert of shifting sands'. As music became more chromatic, its harmonies slithered about with less and less sense of direction. Schoenberg realized that this was no

THE TWENTIETH CENTURY 183

basis for building structures in sound. As he was conscious of a German heritage, to build sonal structures was what he wanted to do. He realized that music had for centuries been using more and more of the 12 notes of the Western music vocabulary in its melodic phrases, and piling up more and more of them in its harmony.

To give a few examples. The middle movement of Bach's *Brandenburg Concerto no. 1* employed what timid academicians termed 'false relations':

Mozart's *Musical Joke* K.522 ends in the following clash of keys, in imitation of a village band:

which could be played on the piano like this:

which is as dissonant as any 20th century music and explodes the naive idea that modern music is modern because it is dissonant.

Berlioz's 'Evocation of Mephistopheles' in his *Damnation of Faust* opens like this:

Liszt's *Faust Symphony* opens with a series of all twelve notes:

And Richard Strauss's fugue in *Thus spake Zarathustra* is another case of the melodic use of all 12 notes:

All these examples were remarkable because exceptional. Schoenberg sought to make the exception the rule.

Now we give an example from Schoenberg's 5 Piano Pieces, op. 23 (1923):

Schoenberg's idea was that a basic series of the twelve notes could be made the structural principle of the new music: that is, his dodecaphonic music would be built out of restatements of the basic series of notes in melodic and/or harmonic formation. The intention was that variety should be achieved by sometimes presenting the basic row in inversion, in retrograde or in retrograde inversion; or in pitch transpositions of any or all of these. But the fundamental 'problematic' German character of the music was taken for granted as its psychological basis: in other words the ethos of late Wagner was accepted. Schoenberg's words to Rufer sound very strange today – the idea of perpetuating German hegemony for another century. This was an odd idea for an Austrian Jew to have! And the rise of Hitler in the very year in which Schoenberg uttered those words – 1922 – was history at its most ironic. Schoenberg's dodecaphony, in comparison to Wagner's post-Tristan music, stands in much the same relation that the so-called planned economy of 20th century social democracy does to 19th century capitalism. In other words, we are presented with a shoring up of decay. Because Schoenberg was a genius, he was able to achieve remarkable things even under self-imposed restrictions. Evidence of this is in his Variations for Orchestra, op. 31. Even so, two of Schoenberg's major works – the oratorio *Die Jakobsleiter* (*Jacob's Ladder*) (begun 1913) and the opera *Moses and Aron* (begun 1931) – remained incomplete after having been begun in the

G

composer's middle age; and this seems to indicate that twelve-note technique was a Procrustean bed upon which Schoenberg's genius was tortured. These incomplete large works also seem to indicate the self-defeating laboriousness of creating large forms in twelve-note technique.

This idea gains support when one realizes that of the two operas by Schoenberg's pupil, Alban Berg (1885–1935), the first, *Wozzeck* (composed 1914–21), was not a twelve-note work and was completed; but the second, *Lulu* (begun 1929) *was* a twelve-note work and was unfinished in full score, though completed in sketch. A letter from Berg to Schoenberg, written on 7 August 1930, admits the laboriousness of composing in twelve-note technique: 'of my new opera I can only report that I am still in the first act. Apart from the composition, *the twelve-note system of which does not permit me to work quickly*, it is the libretto that holds me up so much,' (My italics – R.S.)

Schoenberg's other outstanding pupil, Anton von Webern (1883–1945), even went beyond Schoenberg in strict adherence to the dogma of twelve-note composition and refined on it, but he restricted himself to small forms.

Berg and Webern developed different aspects of Schoenberg: Berg, the super-charged emotional aspect; Webern, the preoccupation with form and technique. Schoenberg's world is one of pentateuchal passion, fanaticism, dedication. He laboured to build Mount Sinai in Berlin and Vienna and sought the Promised Land in California. Berg's world, by contrast, was contemporary; his operatic subjects – a poor soldier, a prostitute. He is both brutal realist and tender lyricist. He tries to wed the abstract and the concrete, tone-rows and folk-tunes. He is compassionate. He pities social rejects. But nothing in his operatic treatment of proletarian characters would lead one to suspect that Berg lived in an age when working people in some countries were on the march. He paints them as totally pathetic and crude. Webern's world, on the other hand, is the sonic equivalent of the cosmology of the microscope. He writes studies in isolated sounds. Refined musicians can here find much revealed in little. But the sonorous stuff, patterned with holes of silence, is too fragile for mass consumption.

The abstraction of dodecaphony induces a cosmopolitan style, though sometimes national characteristics can co-exist with it, as they do in the music of such 'second generation' Schoenberg pupils as the Catalan-born (later British) Roberto Gerhard (1896–1970), the Greek Nikos Skalkottas (1904–49), and the Italian, Luigi Dallapiccola (b. 1904), who, though not a Schoenberg pupil, approached dodecaphony through studying the music of the Schoenberg school. In each case, a national element is manifested by reference to tonality, which creates a contradiction to the dogma of dodecaphony.

Schoenberg himself wrote tonal works at different periods of his life; and he wisely declared that a great deal of music remained to be written 'in C major'. Most of his followers have ignored this. The point is that mediocrity is *exposed* in the familiar idiom of tonal composition, whereas mediocrity is *disguised* in the relatively unfamiliar idiom of dodecaphonic composition. Schoenberg's attitude to tonality is ambivalent, but such ambivalence is preferable to the exclusive postures of his 'followers'. Schoenberg also showed ambivalence in his attitude to religion and politics: he was a Christian, then later an orthodox Jew; and he was first uninterested in politics, then vehemently anti-Nazi (as in his music with speaker *Survivor from Warsaw*).

In 1942 the French composer Olivier Messiaen (b. 1909) set his pupils (including Pierre Boulez) exercises in total serialization. This extends the Schoenbergian principle of a serialized note-row to serialization of rhythm, timbre and intensity. (Serialization of timbre is, of course, only possible between different instruments.) Messiaen himself in 1949 wrote a study for piano, *Mode de valeurs et d'intensités*, which, in its rigidly applied principles, is very different from his mystical/erotic, Scriabin-like *Turangalila* Symphony of 1948. Total serialization became fashionable in Western Europe's sophisticated music circles in the 1950's, but its extreme laboriousness guaranteed that it would be short-lived. It was only to be expected that somebody would think of total serialization, because, over the centuries, each of music's elements at some time has been explored exhaustively. The evolutionary exploration of harmony was outlined in Chapter 2 and the evolutionary extension of melody (to include all twelve notes of the Western semitonal scale) has been traced in the present chapter. Towards the end of Chapter 12, an example of five-beat rhythm was instanced in the music of Reicha, a composer born 200 years ago; further examples of irregular rhythms proliferated towards the end of the 19th century, particularly in Russian music. Around 1900 Percy Grainger was experimenting with composition in free rhythm, suggested to him by performances of folk singers. His *Hill Song* and *Train Music*, orchestral works both dating from the early years of the present century, were notated in multiple time-signatures: 4 beats to the bar, followed by 3, 4½, 2, 5, 7 and so on. Grainger's friend Cyril Scott requested Grainger's permission to use these free rhythms in his Piano Sonata op. 66 (published in 1909 and extensively played over Europe about that time). The next outstanding work to utilize these free rhythms was Stravinsky's *Rite of Spring* (1913). The West German composer Boris Blacher (born in China in 1903) became the leading exponent of additive rhythms (for instance, a 1-beat bar, a 2-beat bar, a 3-beat bar, and so on). So by 1942 the time was ripe for Messiaen to think of total serialization of all music's elements. Even Stravinsky finally embraced serialism.

When the fabric of music becomes subjected to such a degree of organization, there is no room for the human element, emotion. If music is totally organized, patterns on paper become more important than the *sound* of the stuff. The West German, Karlheinz Stockhausen (b. 1928) published his *Piano Piece no. 2* in 1954. To take only one case out of the many which abound in this piece, it contains a chord in which the pianist is expected to play five notes with his right hand with four different intensities: moderately loud, loud, very loud and extremely loud. This is simply unplayable by a human hand, whether the person attached to it is called Smith or Horowitz. But though not playable by a pianist, it is playable on electronic oscillators, which can produce a seemingly limitless variety of rhythmic, melodic, harmonic and contrapuntal complexities in a vast range of timbre and intensity. So the next step after total serialization was electronic music. Stockhausen, for instance, has occupied himself more and more with electronic music, receiving approbation from an esoteric clique (he has even been called 'the greatest composer since Beethoven') but also receiving opposition from audiences and from another West German composer, Hans Werner Henze (b. 1926), who has described Stockhausen as practising a Nazi-like sadism on his audience by inflicting a degree of volume sometimes painful to the ears.

Henze himself has dissociated himself from West Germany by living in Italy. He began as a dodecaphonist but abandoned this method of composition, preferring a freer approach. His five Symphonies trace the emergence of a creative character working its way through the influences of Straussian orchestration and Stravinskyan rhythms. He has also composed operas which have attracted much attention. On revisiting West Germany in the late 1960's, he has been disenchanted by the morale of the country, finding the rise of neo-Nazism particularly revolting. His later work has become more politically motivated and has found expression in a new interest in choral music. Much of this is written for amateurs and children and owes some allegiance to the school of music of the outstanding German pedagogue composer, Carl Orff (b. 1895), who has brought a refreshing naiveté into choral music in his *Carmina Burana*. In 1969 Henze left Europe to live in Cuba. In 1970 he returned to Europe and declared his Marxism in a remarkable interview in *The Observer*.

The difference between ordinary instruments and an electronic oscillator is in the way the sound vibrations are produced. In an ordinary instrument, sounds are produced by percussion, breath or bowing, and result in tremors of the drum head or the strings, frame, reeds or air columns. In an electronic oscillator, these tremors are oscillations of an electronic current. The oscillations are converted, amplified and fed into speakers. The speakers transform them into sound waves. One of the earliest experiments in electrical music was the Telharmonium or the Dynamophone, the invention of an American scientist, Dr. Thaddeus Cahill in 1906. This was almost a musical power station. It used alternating-current generators which produced pure sounds (sounds without overtones, or 'sinusoidal' sound). By a system of switches, these pure sounds were combined to produce notes of any timbre. In 1906 there was neither amplifier nor loudspeaker; only the early telephone. Cahill devised his Telharmonium for telephone lines, so that subscribers could have unusual music when 'holding the line'. The invention was so bulky that it had to be housed in a specially built shed. It was larger than a pipe organ. It would have taken forty railway trucks to transport it. But it only produced whispering sounds: a whispering giant. It attracted the interest of Busoni who wrote about it in his *New Aesthetic* in 1906. But it, perhaps understandably, attracted no commercial attention.

Not until the advent of electronics and, with it, electronic valves and valve amplifiers were new paths opened.

One of the most spectacular pioneers of electronic music was the Soviet scientist, Leon Thérémin, who developed his Théréminvox in 1920. The idea originated in Thérémin setting up his radio capacitometer on his table and disturbing the surrounding atmosphere by moving his fingers. The instrument 'interpreted' this as variations in density and responded with an almost musical sound. The Théréminvox had two valve oscillators: one of variable, the other of fixed, frequency. A capacitor plate in the variable-frequency oscillator was connected to the aerial. Hand movement near the aerial changed the frequency of the oscillator. This frequency was combined with that of the fixed-frequency oscillator. Two different frequencies were then produced: one the sum of the two original frequencies, the other the difference. These 'beat frequencies' covered a wide pitch range. As the loudspeaker had not yet been invented, Thérémin used a giant earphone with a paper horn fitted into it to amplify the sounds. The volume was controlled by a foot-pedal. Thérémin gave public concerts on his Théréminvox and gave a performance before Lenin in 1921. In the mid-Twenties the invention was improved by the addition of a loudspeaker.

Electrical power was also applied to conventional instruments, as in the Hammond organ, the invention of a Chicago watchmaker, Louis Hammond, who took Cahill's idea as his starting-point. In the Thirties, the electric guitar followed and the Neo-Bechstein electric piano. Then the tape recorder and computer-music. Studios for electronic music were set up after World War II in Milan (directed by Berio) and Cologne (directed by Stockhausen).

Most electronic music so far is of the 'bubble and squeak' variety – explorations of fragmented noise or of sound-effects more than sound. The 'bubble and squeak' variety of electronic music is not the *only* one, though: the Dutch composer Henk Badings has composed electronic music with long, unfragmented melodic lines. The idea of including noise within the terms of music is debatable. Noises in the sense of instruments of indefinite pitch – tuneless instruments such as the bass drum and cymbals and so on – have always played a subsidiary role in music. But the idea of bringing this background into the foreground is another matter. Perhaps it is only to be expected in an age of pollution, in which not only rivers are polluted but the very air is – and not only with smoke but with transistor radios which begin to infest beaches and countryside and aeroplane sonic-booms which invade our homes. One of the pioneers of electronic music was the French-American, Edgar Varèse (1886–1965), whose initial impulse to explore these sounds was encouraged by Busoni. Varèse's *Poeme Electronique* (1957–8) was performed as part of the spectacle of sound and light at the Brussels World Fair of 1958 in the pavilion designed by Le Corbusier. Such a *milieu* is the proper setting for these sounds.

Another cognate medium to electronic music is *musique concrète*, which enjoyed a brief vogue in the Fifties. This is tape-recorded and electronically treated natural noise. Its raw material is any noise heard in the workaday world. Previously unheard noises can be produced by recording, for instance, at retarded speed (and therefore at lower pitch) say a railway train's whistle; or recording, say, a fog-horn at an accelerated speed and consequent higher pitch. The difference between *musique concrète* and electronic music is that the 'concrete' kind is based on electronic treatment of non-electronic sound-sources, whereas electronic music is based on electronically generated sound-sources. But both are subject to abstract organization which finds its impulse not in a spontaneous, emotional response to a stimulus in society or nature but in a process of complex calculation which negates or diminishes emotive response.

An inevitable reaction to totally organized serial and/or electronic music was the movement which bears the rather cumbersome name of 'aleatoric' music, that is, random or chance music. Typical of this kind of music (if it can be called music at all) is the composition of separate motives which the performer is invited to play in any order that takes his fancy. Sometimes the performer is even expected to improvise on the minimal material supplied. This is clearly a case of the abdication of the composer, assuming that he was even a composer to begin with.

In the Sixties, Western concert halls became the platforms for 'happenings': quasi-theatrical spectacles which outraged the middle-aged. Perhaps the spectacle of elderly people being outraged was enjoyed by the youthful sectors of the audiences even more than the 'happening' itself. Sometimes even sex is dragged into these 'performances'. Certainly, *music* seems the last consideration. The American John Cage is for some Western youths a cultural hero or anti-hero. He has the distinction of sitting at a piano with a stop-watch, timing a certain period of silence and being applauded for thereby having created a 'new composition'. The 'music', we are told, is in the accidental sounds heard in the silence. Cage represents a religious, rather than a musical, movement. He is a professed Zen-Buddhist. Evidently, modern life is too much for some young people who take to Cage as they take to drugs. Cage has toured American and European Universities, delivering a lecture literally entitled 'Lecture on Nothing'. But his followers are only a minority of the student population.

The great majority of Western youth prefer the world of 'pop' music or of 'folk'. 'Pop' is part of the world of consumer goods. It is slung at modern youth, not only in records, but in fashion. Youth is the victim. If they are aware of being victimized, they still say they enjoy it – so what? The Beatles were a business syndicate for the manufacture of songs, records and fashions. Their cultural orientation was vaguely towards lower-middle-class liberalism. Some Western musicologists have taken them seriously and written analyses of their songs, analyses incomprehensible to Beatles fans.

'Folk' differs from folk music (without inverted commas) in so far as it is made by the performer or by a contemporary performer rather than by some anonym from the past. The outstanding exponent of 'folk' is the American Bob Dylan, who is a poet of perception and a musician of versatility (he plays guitar – both acoustic and electric, harmonica, piano and auto-harp). He has composed songs of protest and love songs. He claims to be no singer but 'hollers' his songs in the tradition of the Whitmanesque 'barbaric yawp', which was extended in the tramp poetry of the American Vachel Lindsay and the Russian Mayakovsky, and the singing of 'Leadbelly', Woody Guthrie and Pete Seeger. By combining 'rock' music with 'folk' (that is urban rhythm with country song) and by going over to the electric guitar, Dylan at first incensed some of his fans who preferred his earlier, simpler style; but, in making the change, he has reached a vast audience. He is too serious a poet/composer/performer to need to resort to such gimmicks as erotic contortions with the microphone. He is a progressive influence on youth today.

Though 'pop' and 'folk' singers occupy the limelight, the nineteenth century prima donna no longer takes pride of place in music culture. Fifty years ago, Melba and Caruso enjoyed transatlantic voyages and arrived in New York or London relaxed and in fine voice. Nowadays, opera stars go by jet and arrive half dead. Even the virtuoso pianist has been eclipsed by the conductor, who might be called the 'primo uomo' of modern music. Conductors in general are the most mediocre of musicians. A good orchestra can play well *in spite of* a conductor, though a conductor of genius can transform a good orchestra into a superlative one. In my view, the great conductors of our epoch are: Toscanini, Furtwängler, Walter and Stokowski. Among the younger conductors, Bernstein is outstanding, probably because like most of those of the older generation, he is also a composer and performer of formidable and versatile talent whose conducting is informed with creativity. The Soviet conductor Rozhdestvensky directs his orchestra with consummate, almost Toscanini-like, control; and is the only conductor I have ever seen who has held up the score he has conducted for the composer *in absentia* to be applauded.

The 'spectacular' symphony concert has become a part of middle-class social-life, but the song recital, which enjoyed such a vogue in the Twenties, is almost extinct. The song recital is the most *personal* form of music-making: its continuation was bound to be difficult when life became more *impersonal*. But such a fine body of song as, for instance was created in the Twenties by the British composers George Butterworth, Roger Quilter, John Ireland, Granville Bantock, Bernard van Dieren, Peter Warlock, Norman Peterkin and others, deserves a recrudescence.

Re-reading what I've written, I am aware of omissions. I have missed out Georges Enesco, the great Rumanian nationalist composer who was also a virtuoso violinist and fine pianist and the teacher of Menuhin. I should have said something too about the French composers, Fauré and Roussel, two fastidious masters in the classical mould; and about another Frenchman, Koechlin, a many-sided genius. I might have said something about the Italian nationalist composers, Pizzetti, Malipiero and Casella, and something about Tippett and Walton, who have contributed notably to British music. The connoisseurs of the British symphony would expect me to mention Rubbra, Simpson, Bernard Stevens and William Wordsworth. The reader will be able to augment my self-criticism. To say that such omissions are inevitable in a book of this kind, which, after all, is only an *introduction* to the subject, is not to lessen regret.

As I come to the end of my observations on the music of the present century, I am forced to reflect on the impact of two world wars which seem to have sent the arts temporarily berserk. The line of continuity has been broken. If progress towards more human awareness is to be made it can only be made by continuing the tradition of what is good in the past. Wholesale jettisoning of past culture is unproductive and merely a histrionic gesture of futility. The seeds of our age were sown in the 19th century. Significant developments in our century had their inception a hundred years ago: technology, Darwinism and Marxism, for instance. These things have gone on developing, not without struggle and mistakes, and have increased human awareness. The art movements of the last century have gone on developing too; but the cancer of commercial monopoly and the race of fashion have often obscured this fact. The English nonagenarian composer,

15 Towards World Music

... and to win freedom is its destiny

In the first chapter we considered the separate development of music's elements on different continents: the development of rhythm in Africa, melody in India, and harmony and polyphony in the West. In the main body of the book, we have considered the alternating phases, the ebb and flow, of polyphony and harmony in the history of Western music. In our final chapter, we consider the emergence of a new concept of world music, to which all other musics have been preparatory.

Western culture is – a few isolated pockets excepted – like a worked mine. Europe is tired. Western art must look to the East. It is already doing so, as we shall see in this chapter.

The aeroplane and television have intensified and accelerated inter-continental communications. The world is shrinking. As it shrinks, the inter-traffic of cultures is bound to grow. Kipling's adage about the mutual exclusiveness of East and West is being proved wrong. As Paul Robeson has said, 'There are many nations, but there is only one race: the human race'. Music – the great harmony – is one, as the human race is one. As humanity achieves unity – not without difficulty – music will achieve unity also, because it reflects reality; or rather, the inherent unity of music will be realized. In the African jungle, rhythm is born free because it is made by people whose nudity frees them from the inhibitions of so-called civilized man, who is as under-vitalized as he is over-clothed. But music has lost its primeval freedom because man has lost his. Music is like a bastard child who is free to laugh and play until it is old enough to hear what bastardy is. And freedom is not re-won without struggle. But this is a subjective analogy: we must widen it to embrace the world, for music is a world. The primeval freedom of African rhythm is incomplete freedom, because it is achieved by the emphasis of only one aspect of music. The birth-right of music's freedom has been lost with humanity's freedom; it will be re-won when African rhythm pulsates with Indian melody and when Western harmony and polyphony add new dimensions to Afro-Asian music. This idea will naturally shock the timid. It is already coming about, all the same.

In 1897 the fifteen-year old Australian Percy Grainger, studying music in Frankfurt, was advised by his professor of piano to enter for the Mendelssohn Scholarship. Grainger wondered whether, if he won it, he would be allowed to use the prize-money to go to China to study Chinese music. The professor disapproved: 'Certainly not! The Mendelssohn Scholarship is not awarded to idiots!' At that time the idea of Teutonic hegemony was so ingrained in European music circles that no music was considered worthy if it did not conform to German models; and this situation was even accepted in countries other than Germany. Grainger didn't win the scholarship and never went to China, but he did later study Chinese music in collaboration with the American musicologist Joseph Yasser. The Grainger MSS Collection in the Library of Congress includes a setting of a Chinese folksong 'harmonized by Joseph Yasser and pianized (a characteristic Graingerism! – R.S.) by Percy Grainger'.

The German professor's rebuff didn't daunt Grainger. In 1898 he composed an *Eastern Intermezzo* for small orchestra, which grew out of his keen interest in Oriental music, stemming from his familiarity with Chinese and Japanese music heard in his early childhood in Australia. But perhaps Grainger's most significant piece that relates to Oriental music in a subtle way, not by employing any of the hall-marks of Eastern music but by being conceived almost exclusively in single-line-melody with next to no chords, was composed in 1908. This piece has an unusual title: *Arrival Platform Humlet* (which the composer explains as the kind of thing he might hum on a railway platform!) This title should not obscure the serious nature and inventiveness of the music. It carries invention so far as to create an a-thematic melody free from all but the most minimal repetition. It begins:

Ex 111 With healthy and somewhat fierce "go"
mp somewhat pertly

and it contains such an unpredictable phrase as this:

Ex 112

This may come as a surprise to music lovers who know Grainger only by his popular trifles. I am not making out a case for him as an 'important figure': fortunately he avoided the bane of the 'important' – especially in the Teutonic sense. But the present century has had no greater indicator of future possibilities in music. If he 'cocks a snook' at tradition, and bids a merry farewell to the past, with the other hand he indicates the future. Best of all, Grainger was a true democrat in music who broke with the European cult of the aristocratic artist and who went out among people to make his music, consorting with primitives and amateurs.

In June 1913 Bela Bartók collected Arabian folk-music in Algeria. These researches influenced such compositions as his *Danse Orientale* for piano (composed in December 1913) and his *Chant arabe*, no. 42 of his *44 Duos* for two violins (1931).

Natalie Curtis, an American pupil of Busoni, in 1907 published the results of her research into Red Indian music in *The Indians' Book* (Harper, N.Y.). In 1910 she introduced Busoni to Red Indian musicians in Columbus, Ohio. Five years later Busoni brought out three compositions based on Natalie Curtis's researches and on his own experience of the Red Indian way of life and thought: the *Red Indian Diary* for piano, the *Indian Fantasy* for piano and orchestra and *Song of the Spirit Dance* for small orchestra. The roots of Red Indian culture go back to the emanation of this people from the Far East. Even today it is their Mongoloid features which unite Red Indians racially. Latest radio-carbon tests, measuring the age of charcoal deposits by their remaining radioactivity, indicate that the original American Indian, starting from Siberia and crossing into Alaska, had penetrated to New Mexico 20,000 years ago. So the music of the Red Indian is Far Eastern in origin. Though he was a consummator of European culture, Busoni had aspirations as an innovator and independently realized the truth of what Sir Herbert Read expressed when he wrote, 'We can learn more of the essential nature of art from its earliest manifestations in primitive man (and in children) than from its intellectual elaboration in great periods of culture'.

Busoni pursued his attempted coalescence of Oriental and Occidental musics in his opera *Turandot*, which, written in 1917, precedes Puccini's opera of the same name. Busoni uses some genuine Chinese folk-tunes in his opera and his treatment shows a structural grasp of the five Chinese pentatonic modes.

Already in his essay *Towards a New Aesthetic of Music* (1906) Busoni had adumbrated an extension of the European major/minor tonal system by the introduction of new 7-note scales selected from the twelve semitones. His claim that there are 113 such scales is an understatement: there are actually 150. These scales – for example, C – D flat – E flat – F flat – G – A – B – C, or C – D – E flat – F flat – G – A sharp – B – C – relate to the Hindu raga-principle explained in our first chapter.

At Busoni's suggestion, the French composer Maurice Emmanuel composed a *Sonatina* on Hindu modes in 1920. The following quotation shows the new lyricism and unusual (but logical) harmony resulting from the Hindu mode employed:

Ex 113
Tempo di Walzer

Emmanuel's pupil Olivier Messiaen, the leading French composer of today, has extended his teacher's interest in Indian music, as may be seen from a comparative study of Messiaen's *Cantéyodjayâ* for piano (1953) and Emmanuel's *Hindu Sonatina*.

In Eastern Europe microtonal music can sometimes be heard from folk-musicians. To trace the ethnographic origins of such phenomena as microtones is an involved operation necessitating knowledge, not only of racial characteristics, but also of ancient trade routes; but there can be little doubt that the microtones of East European music relate to the microtones of Indian music. The Czech composer Alois Hába (born 1893), as a boy, used to play the violin with his father and two elder brothers at folk festivals. His sense of 'absolute pitch' (that is, his innate ability to identify the pitch of any note heard) told him that the East-Moravian folk-singers sang in quarter-tones and sixth-tones. Mature reflection on this experience suggested to Hába the possibility of using these microtones as the bases for musical composition. In 1927, after practising such composition for some years, he formulated his theory in a treatise. He also practised non-thematic composition – a development of the technique employed by Grainger in examples 111 and 112 – and also published a book on this subject in 1923. In order to write down his microtonal music, Hába had to invent a notation. Here is an example from his 11th Quartet, op. 87 (1957/58):

Hába has also designed and supervised the construction of a quarter-tone piano.

In 1925 the Polish-American composer-pianist, Leopold

Godowsky, published his mammoth *Java Suite* for piano, which plays for approximately 45 minutes. A well-seasoned globe-trotter, he was captivated by the Island of Java, the fabled 'Garden of the East', the most densely populated island in the world. Much as he marvelled at the beauties of its tropical vegetation, its huge volcanoes and majestic, ancient ruins, his profoundest impression was of the native music, *Gamelan*, played on indigenous instruments, mainly consisting of percussion made of metal, wood and bamboo, augmented by bells, chimes, gongs, sounding boards, bowls, pans, drums (some barrel-like), tom-toms, native xylophones, and the sonorous, aeolian harp-like *alang-alang*. The only string instrument in the ensemble is the ancient, guitar-shaped *rebab*, which is played in the manner of the lute. Godowsky found the *Gamelan* sonority 'so weird, spectral, fantastic and bewitching' that he imagined himself 'in a realm of enchantment'. He goes on to describe it as 'a perfume of sound... a musical breeze'. In the first movement of his *Java Suite* he attempts to recreate *Gamelan* sonority in terms of the piano:

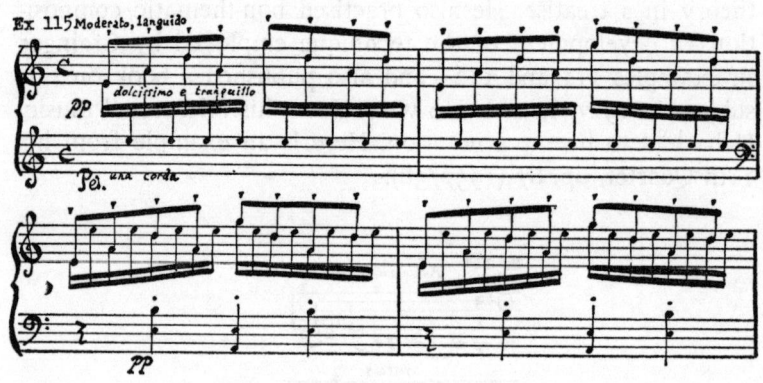

Debussy and Bartók also wrote works influenced by Javanese music. Later composers, such as Pierre Boulez in his *Pli selon pli* (1962), have produced orchestral scores influenced by the sound of *Gamelan*, sometimes introducing exotic percussion including large sheets of metal.

The greatest Polish composer since Chopin – Karol

Szymanowski (1882–1937), devoted a major part of his output to settings of Persian poets. It is of particular interest to read the opinion of the Parsi composer Kaikhosru Shapurji Sorabji on Szymanowski's Third Symphony, 'Song of the Night' (composed 1914–16), which is a setting (for tenor and chorus with orchestra) from the Divàn of Jullàl-ùddin Rùmi, the great mystical poet of Iran: 'Around this poem, Szymanowski has written music of a radiant purity of spirit, of an elevated ecstasy of expression, music so permeated with the very essence of the choicest and rarest specimens of Iranian art – the whole score glows with gorgeous colour, rich, yet never garish nor crude, like a Persian painting or silk rug – that such a feat is unparalleled in Western Music.'

Sorabji's own compositions present Occidental and Oriental aspects. Born of a Parsi father and a Spanish-Sicilian mother, he has lived most of his life in England. The following statement is his answer to the questions that his work and his self-imposed ban on its performance inevitably arouse: 'I am not a "modern" composer in the inverted commas sense. I utterly and indignantly repudiate the epithet as being in any way applicable to me. I write very long, very elaborate works that are entirely alien and antipathetic to the fashionable tendencies prompted, publicised and plugged by the various "establishments" revolving around this or that modern composer. Why do I neither seek nor encourage performance of my works? Because they are neither intended for, nor suitable for it under present, or indeed any foreseeable conditions: no performance at all is vastly preferable to an obscene travesty.'

Opus Clavicembalisticum for piano (1930) heads the long list of Sorabji's later marathon works which include orchestral and choral, as well as chamber music. It plays for 2½ hours and is cast in three sections. Part One contains an Introduction, Chorale Prelude, Fugue and Fantasy; Part Two contains a double Fugue, and Interlude (consisting of a theme and 48 variations), a Cadenza and a triple Fugue; and Part Three contains a second Interlude (consisting of Toccata, Adagio and Passacaglia with 81 variations), a second Cadenza, a quadruple Fugue and a Coda. This music is seldom overtly Oriental.

Its Orientalism is found in its fantastic intricacy of structure and ornament more than in any apparent exoticism; but occasionally a passage is deeply dyed with Oriental colour. One aspect of Sorabji's music is its rich sensuousness. Another is its austerity, manifest in complex fugal writing which sometimes makes the pages of his piano music resemble those of a full score! After a careful study of his later compositions (some consulted in manuscript), I would say that his *forte* is his rhapsodic vein, which is phenomenal in its volubility and invention.

The American composer, Henry Cowell (1897–1964), was interested in the music of Iran, after visiting that country towards the end of his life. He composed a *Homage to Iran* which even employs Iranian instruments. There is, of course, no logical reason why the European symphony orchestra should be the ultimate organization of massed instruments.

In the 1960's Benjamin Britten composed three 'parables' influenced by Japanese *Nō* plays. The music was expressed in an even greater economy of material than in Britten's previous work, melodic lines employed the free *glissandi* (gliding or swooping of pitch) and the percussion-writing was influenced by the exotic tintinnabulations of Japanese music. The first of Britten's 'parables' was *Curlew River* which transmuted a Far Eastern, Buddhist legend into a Western, Christian ideology; the second, *The Burning Fiery Furnace*, was based on an Old Testament story of a Jewish resistance movement; the third was *The Prodigal Son*. This trilogy marked a new departure by the composer whose *Peter Grimes* (1945) created a new era in English opera.

Probably no-one has been more aware of the need for the establishment of world culture – or has laboured more for its parturition – than has Rabindranath Tagore, the Bengali poet (1861–1941). His founding of the first international university at Santiniketan, near Calcutta, in the aftermath of World War I, embodied his ideal. He was perhaps the first Indian to embrace Western culture, though he retained his Indian identity. His creative gifts as a composer are not so well known as his poetic genius, but he composed many melodies to his own poems, often to songs in his plays. A scholar of the *ragas* and of Sanskrit song, his preferred mode of expression was in the idiom of Bengali folk-song. Here is an example notated from Tagore's singing in 1924 and transcribed and translated into English by his disciple, Dr. Arthur Geddes:

A century after Tagore's birth, the Indian *sitar*-player, Ravi Shankar, has done much to increase appreciation of Indian music in the West, particularly in Britain. (The *sitar* is India's most popular string instrument, made from a seasoned gourd and teak.) Shankar has collaborated with Yehudi Menuhin, who is a persuasive advocate of Asian music in the West.

Writing in the Israeli music magazine, *Bat Kol*, in 1960, the Israeli composer, Mordechai Seter, speculated on problems of world music. Taking Israel as the most Easternly outpost of the West and the most Westernly outpost of the East, he voiced his conviction that his country may well qualify geographically as the melting-point of world music (Spain and Sicily are also melting-points of different cultures.) Seter also thought that world music could be encouraged by composers writing in those forms which are common to both Eastern and Western musics, such as passacaglia-form and variation-form.

Another contemporary Israeli composer who has occupied himself with Eastern music is the Kodály pupil, Oedoen Partos. In his chamber music he has employed the Arab scale-technique of *maqam*, by which the scalic inflexions undergo continuous variation.

In the People's Republic of China, contemporary Chinese musicians have applied European techniques to their indigenous music. A simple demonstration of this in embryo is seen in a piano piece by Ho Lu-ting, entitled *The Shepherd's Pipe* (1950). The melody of this piece is based on Chinese folk-song and its counterpoint is modelled on the European form of the two-part Invention:

The emergence of new African States has been accompanied by an awakening of interest in national culture. An example of this is the publication of an outstanding piece of research, *Folk Songs of Ghana* by J. H. Kwabena Nketia, published by the University of Ghana in 1963. The copious music examples are preceded by discussion of social background, musical and poetic structure, accompaniment, method of performance and dancing. The book is expressly designed 'to provide source material for performers, composers and students of African music'. Such a volume applies and extends European and American techniques of ethno-musicology and is bound to advance the cause of African music both in Africa and elsewhere.

Invaluable work on native South African music has been done by the scholar, Percival Kirby, and the field-worker Hugh Tracy. Kirby has published the definitive book on the musical instruments of South Africa, rich in anecdote and the observation of personal experience, and masterly in method. Tracy has recorded much of the indigenous music and has also filmed the ritualistic dancing which it accompanies.

The English composer, Alan Bush (born 1900), has used Tracy's recordings as a basis for *Three African Sketches* (1960) for flute and piano. Bush has also written *Three Raga Melodies* (1961) for solo violin.

In my own *Passacaglia on DSCH* (1962) for piano, dedicated to Dmitry Shostakovich, one passage is based on the actual experience of hearing a South African tribal drummer play 15 drums in one performance. I attempted to capture the drum sonority by striking the bass strings of the piano with the left palm while playing on the keyboard with the right hand. In John Ogdon's recording of this work for HMV, experiments with microphone placing further helped to recreate the 'African' sonority.

All the examples I have given in this chapter are cases of Western composers employing aspects or techniques of Eastern or African music, or Eastern composers using something from Western music. But I believe that the future will see – or rather, hear – musical multilingualism, analagous to the polyglot poetry which has already been written by Ezra Pound, Hugh MacDiarmid and others. This music will wait, as truth waits, to be discovered. It cannot be forced.

A crude misunderstanding of this adumbration of world music would be made if an enthusiast played on one record-player a disc of African drum-music and, at the same time, on another record-player, a disc of a Hindu raga-singer or a Chinese bamboo-pipe-player, and then were to accompany these by improvised European harmony on the piano or on a guitar. Such an experiment might amuse. It might confuse. It would bring world music no nearer. It would be abortive because it would take abstraction as a basis: it would abstract from different musics in the hope of achieving synthesis. But synthesis can only be achieved through the whole process of life and experience. The experiment just described would be dangerously misleading for an amateur. It might be a useful exercise for an experienced composer. He might learn something about relationships and balance:

he might, for instance, learn how a highly ornamented melody does not complement frenetic rhythm and that complex harmony needs simple rhythm and melody; and so on. But, as yet, professional Western musicians know as little of Eastern music as Western laymen know of Western music. World music will be born when West and East come together as its begetters, when musicians really know something of different cultures.

African music is primarily rhythmic and physical; Asian is primarily melodic and spiritual; and European music is primarily harmonic and polyphonic, emotional and intellectual. The sum of the physical, the spiritual, the emotional and intellectual, is the whole being of an individual's life. So the sum of world music is the complete music of mankind.

Goethe spoke of 'world citizenship'. Such a concept implies the necessity of world music. No 'world citizen' can go on thinking that the Viennese classics of the 18th century reflect his world view.

Some clever young people, fresh from university, enjoy throwing an abstruse word into such an argument as this: I can hear them say, with their gay cynicism: 'There is nothing in the *morphology* of Occidental and Oriental musics to suggest any fusion'. And that is intended to close the discussion. Then perhaps a lecturer or professor might quietly remind us that Eastern music is static where Western music is motoric. And I would agree. But I would point out that art, like life, is full of contradiction and the epic artist functions at the point where extremes meet.

The epic artist ... he is the crux of the argument. The historic events of the 20th century are epic, and only epic art can reflect their reality. And music confined to the culture of one nation or one continent cannot be truly epic. Only that music can be epic which is created by a musician aware of the unity and conflict of the different musics of different nations and different continents. As a man, he will know that conflict is the law of divided society; but as a musician, he will know that unity is equally a law of that great harmony which is music and which one day will reflect the reality of society united. In that day, both music and man will have re-won their common birthright of freedom.

A Brief Bibliography

RUTLAND BOUGHTON The Reality of Music (*Kegan Paul, London, 1934*)

FERRUCCIO BUSONI A New Aesthetic – in Three Classics in the Aesthetics of Music (*Dover, N.Y. 1964*)

JAQUES CHAILLEY 40,000 Years of Music (*MacDonald, London, 1964*)

WANDA LANDOWSKA Landowska on Music (*Secker & Warburg, London, 1965*)

CARL NEILSON Living Music (*Hutchinson, London, 1953*)

ED. PERCY SCHOLES The Oxford Companion to Music (*Oxford University Press, new edition 1970*)

Acknowledgments

During the final phase of work on this book, Pablo Casals' *Reflections Joys and Sorrows* appeared (MacDonald, London, 1970) and I found in this wise book a confirmation of all that I was trying to say about music and life. I acknowledge his example and shall be content if the spirit of these words of his can be sensed behind my own book: 'Music must serve a purpose; it must be a part of something larger than itself, a part of humanity; and that, indeed, is at the core of my argument with music today — its lack of humanity. A musician is also a man, and more important than his music is his attitude toward life. Nor can the two be separated.' So first, a salute to Casals.

It was, of course, necessary to consult a considerable number of books. I wish to thank Miss Phyllis Hamilton, Librarian of the Music Room, Edinburgh Public Library, and Mr. Michael Anderson, Librarian of the Reid Music Library, University of Edinburgh, for their unfailing courtesy.

Discussions with friends and fellow musicians have been invaluable, especially those with Dr. Alan Bush, Alastair Chisholm, Dr. Andrew Cockburn, Martin Dalby, David Dorward, Gordon Green, Dr. John Guthrie, Lord Patrick Douglas-Hamilton, Leonard Friedman, John Ellis (also the photographer of the author's portrait which appears on the dust jacket), Margaret Holden, Graham Johnson, Charles King, Bernard Langley, John Lazarus, James May, Douglas Miller, John Ogdon, Ates Orga, Norman Peterkin, John Rose, Colin Scott-Sutherland, Dr. Bernard Stevens, Joseph Szigeti, Harold Taylor, Derek Watson, and William Wordsworth.

My book and I have also benefitted from correspondence with musicians overseas, especially Louis Ballard, the late Percy Grainger, and Walter Hartley (all U.S.A.); Professor Grigori Kogan (U.S.S.R.); Luigi Dallapiccola and Roman Vlad (Italy).

I owe much to B.B.C. staff who have produced radio and TV talks of mine and have helped me to express myself succinctly about music. They are: John Amis, Dr. Roger Fiske, John Gray, Denys Gueroult, Hans Keller, Robert Layton, Michael Pope, W. Gordon Smith, and Christopher Sykes.

To my proof-readers Rod. C. MacCulloch and Norman Peterkin I am greatly indebted. The book has also been improved by advice on scientific data from Professor Manfred Gordon and on historical data from Alex. Winton. Whatever errors remain are my own responsibility.

My gratitude also goes to Derek Watson, who compiled the index, and to my son Gordon, who typed it.

I have been fortunate in that my publisher, Morris Kahn, is also a musician. He has been generous over minor differences of opinion.

Finally I wish to thank my wife Marjorie for typing the main body of the book and for many expert suggestions.

Index

acoustics, 27ff, 36
Aeschelus, 30f
Albeniz, 177
Alberti, 67
Albrechtsberger, 133
Alkan, 142
Ambrose, Saint, 38
Andersen, 175
Animuccia, 71
Anfilov, 67
Arcadelt, 71
Aristotle, 31
Aristoxenus, 28
Armstrong, Louis, 172
Arne, 99
ars antiqua, 56
ars nova, 56f
Asafaev, 181
Aston, 25
Auber, 140
Auric, 170
à Wood, 76

Bach, C. P. E., 103, 116, 117, 133
Bach, J. C., 116
Bach, J. C. F., 116
Bach, J. S., 14, 15, 18, 19, 57, 89, 90, 93, 94, 100, 102ff, 128, 146, 169, 170, 183
Bach, V., 111
Bach, W. F., 116
Bacon, F., 68
Bacon, R., 48
Badings, H., 191
Banks, D., 173
Bantock, 194
Balakirev, 157
Ballard, L., 196
Bartók, 103, 131, 154, 169, 175, 178, 179, 199, 202
Beatles, The, 192
Beaumarchais, 130, 154

Bechstein, 12
Bécourt, 139
Beecham, 179
Beethoven, 14, 19, 40, 90, 98, 116, 118, 119ff, 123ff, 133ff, 141, 145, 153, 155, 162, 169, 189
Bekhterev, 8
bel canto, 148
Bellini, 148
Bellman, 138, 156
Bennet, Sterndale, 140
Berg, 181, 186
Berio, L., 191
Berlioz, 14, 89, 96, 135, 142, 144, 147, 156, 158, 159, 161, 184
Bernstein, L., 173, 193
Berwald, 140
Binchois, 60, 62f
Bishop, 140
Bizet, 164
Blacher, B., 188
Bloch, 179
Blow, 89
Boethius, 54f
Bohm, 111
Boito, 156
Bolden, Buddy, 171
Borodin, 157
Boughton, 90
Boulez, P., 187, 202
Bourgault-Ducoudray, 175
Brahms, 15, 21, 144, 145f, 156, 169
Bramante, 67
Brecht, 195
Brian, H., 194f
Britten, B., 90f, 179, 204
Britton, 99f
Brontë, E., 145
Brouwer, L., 196
Browning, R. and E., 144
Brubeck, Dave, 173
Bruckner, 163

Brunelleschi, 67
Bukofzer, M., 52, 53
Bull, 78f, 82
Burney, 135
Burns, 138, 156
Bush, A., 195, 207
Busoni, 7, 8, 17, 130, 169f, 190, 191, 199f
Butterworth, 194
Buxtehude, 111
Byrd, 76f, 78, 82
Byron, 142

Caccini, 14, 83f
Cage, J., 192
Cahill, 189f
Callas, M., 135
Campion, 80
canon, 53, 54, 63
  by augmentation, 63
  by diminution, 63
  'crab', 58
  ennime, 63f
  'mirror', 63
Cardinal, 44
Carl Theodor, Elector, 117
Caruso, 193
catch, 90
Cavalli, 88
concerto, 123
  grosso, 94
counterpoint, 10, 69
Chabrier, 164
Chaliapin, 39, 159
Chambonnières, 113
Chaucer, 48f
Cherubini, 135, 149
Chernyshevsky, 181
Chopin, 14, 20, 90, 108, 114, 128, 144, 147ff, 168, 172, 174, 175
Claude le Jeune, 73
Clementi, 135, 148
Cocteau, 170
Codex, 45
Coleridge-Taylor, 173f
Columbus, 49
Cook, Captn., 137f
Coomaraswamy, 33
Cooper, 132
Copland, A., 178, 181
Corelli, 94
Coster, 49, 66
Couperin, 80, 113f, 117, 146
Couperin (family), 113
Coussemaker, 51
Cowell, 177, 204
Craig, 91
Cramer, 135
Cui, 157

Curtis, N., 174, 199
Cyril and Methodious, 39, 42
Czerny, 135, 140

da capo aria, 94
D'Alembert, 115
Dallapiccola, L., 40, 187
Dankworth, J., 173
Dante, 48f
Danyel, 80
Da Ponte, 130
Dargomizhsky, 157
d'Arras, 44
Darwin, 194
Davis, Miles, 173
Debussy, 80, 154, 167, 168, 169, 202
de Beldemandis, 56
de Bornelh, 45
de Cabezón, 78, 108f
de Handlo, 56
de la Halle, 44
Delibes, 140
De Lisle, 139
Delius, 154, 163, 167, 169
de Marsailles, 43
Democritus, 28
De Muris, 56
de Nesle, 44
Dent, 130
De Pachmann, 172
Des Prez, 64f, 66, 102
de Provins, 45
Descartes, 112
Dett, N., 174
Donizetti, 154f
Dufay, 60, 62f
Duncan, Isadora, 145
de Vaqueiras, 42
de Vigeois, 41
de Vitri, 56, 57
Diaz, 49
di Botta, 87
Diderot, 115
Dimitrov, 66
D'Indy, 169
dissonance, 17ff, 183f
Dobravsky, 152
dodecaphony, 182
Dowland, 80ff, 84
Dryden, 89
Duns Scotus, 48
Dunstaple, 59f, 62, 102
Dürer, 112
Durey, 170
Dušek, F. X., 135
Dušek, J. L., 135
Dvořak, 153
Dylan, Bob, 193

INDEX

East, 76
Ebert, 136
Einstein, 130
Eisler, 195
Eleanor of Aquitaine, 43, 45
Elgar, 169, 179
Elizabeth I, 75
Ellington, Duke, 172f
Emerson, 177
Emmanuel, 16f, 21, 30, 131, 200f
Enesco, 194
Engels, 180
Erasmus, 64
Euler, 101
Evelyn, 48, 99

faburden or fauxbourdon, 52f
Falla, 177, 179
Farnaby, 80
Fauré, 194
Ferrabosco (family), 78
Ferrier, Kathleen, 116
Field, 135, 147f, 150, 157
figured bass, 83 (ex. 52)
Fitzgerald, Ella, 173
Fitzgerald, Scott, 172
Ford, 80
Foster, 156f
Franck, 66, 135, 163
Franklin, 138
Franco of Cologne, 55
Franz, 98
Frauenlob, 46
Frederick the Great, 109, 117
French overture, 88
Froissart, 25
Frescobaldi, 93f
fugue, 79, 112, 113

Gabrieli, A., 73
Gabrieli, G., 73, 93, 133
Gade, 140
Gaforius, 56
Galilei, V., 83
Galileo, 83
Garibaldi, 155
Gastoué, 36
Gay, 99
Geddes, A., 205
George I, 96f
Gerhard, 187
Gershwin, 82, 173, 179
Gesualdo, 74
Gevaert, 30
Gibbons, 78
Gilbert, 142
Glazunov, 175
Glinka, 157
Gluck, 114f, 160

Godowsky, 177, 201f
Goethe, 67, 136, 208
Golias, Bishop, 41
Gorky, 169, 181
Gossec, 123
Gostling, 89
Gounod, 89, 135, 164
Goya, 177
Grainger, 138, 174, 175, 188, 198f, 201
Granados, 177
Gregory I, 36, 49
Grétry, 66
Grieg, 90, 132, 153f, 173, 176
Gropius, 180
ground bass, 91
Guéranger, 40
Guido d'Arezzo, 54f, 56, 60
Guthrie, Woody, 193
gymel, 50, 52, 53

Hába, A., 201
Hahn, 66
Halévy, 147
Hammond, 190
Handel, 89, 90, 94, 95ff, 102, 112, 128
Handy, W. C., 172
Hanslick, 146
harmony, 10, 12, 13f, 15, 16, 20
Harris, J. C., 156
Harris, R., 178
Hauer, 182
Hawkesworth, 138
Haydn, 14, 20, 116, 117, 118, 119ff, 123, 126, 133ff, 148
Helmholtz, 27, 67
Henry V, 75
Henry VI, 75
Henry VIII, 75
Henze, H. W., 189
Herder, 138, 141, 147
Hérold, 140
Hill, Joe, 195
Hindemith, 179f, 181
Hitler, 160, 175, 185
Ho, 206
Hoffman, 144
Holst, 179
homophonic music, 71f, 97
Honneger, 170
Horowitz, 172
Huber, 103
Hucbald, 51, 52
Hugo, 156
Hummel, 135
Humperdink, 162
Humphrey, 89

idée fixe, 161
Idelsohn, 36

INDEX

Ingersoll, 9
Ireland, J., 194
Ives, 177

Janáček, 178f
jazz, 170ff
Jeppesen, K., 19
John XXII, 59
Jongen, 66
Joyce, 175

Kabalevsky, D., 176, 181
Kandinsky, 167
Keiser, 113
Kennedy-Fraser, 148
Kepler, 101
Khachaturian, A., 181
Kilpinen, 174
Kingsley, 140
Kipling, 197
Kirby, P., 206
Kirkpatrick, R., 94, 95
Kodály, 103, 131, 175, 176, 205ff
Koechlin, 194
Kokoshka, 167
Kristensen, 175

Ladré, 138
La Fayette, 138
Lamb, 175
Lambert, 170
Landowska, 114, 115, 177
Lasso, 72
law of inversion of chords, 114f
Lawes, 90
Lawrence, D. H., 123
Le Corbusier, 191
Leibniz, 112
Leitmotif, 161
Lekeu, 66
Lenin, 181, 190
Le Notre, 87
Leonardo, 49, 65, 130
Leoncavallo, 164
Leonin, 54, 56
Lindsay, 193
Linné, 112
Liszt, 14, 57, 79, 90, 128, 135, 142f, 152f, 158, 160, 161, 163, 184
Longo, 94
Lorca, 95
Lortzing, 140
Loyola, 68f
Ludwig II, 161
Lully, 87ff, 94
Lunacharsky, 181
Luther, 46, 68
Lutoslawski, W., 182

MacCormack, 82, 148

MacCrimmon, 25
MacDiarmid, 178, 207
MacDowell, 176, 177
Machaut, 57ff, 102
Maeterlinck, 167
Magellan, 49
Mahler, 163, 167
Malipiero, G. F., 194
Manelli, 86
Manet, 167
Mannheim rocket, 118
Marschner, 141
Martin le Franc, 60
Marco Polo, 48
Marx, 160, 162, 194
Mary, Queen of Scots, 75
Mascagni, 164
Massenet, 140
Mattheson, 113
Mayakovsky, 193
Mayaskovsky, 181
Mazzini, 155
Medtner, 196
Mel, 71
Melba, 193
Melody, 10, 131
Mendelssohn, 98, 100, 140, 145
Menuhin, Y., 194
Merbecke, 90
Merulo, 93
Messiaen, 187, 188, 201
metamorphosis of themes, 161
Meyer, E. H., 182
Meyerbeer, 14, 147, 154, 159, 163f
Michael, Bishop, 39
Michelangelo, 67
Mickiewicz, 151
microtones, 24, 201
Mochnacki, 151
Mocquereau, 40
modes, ecclesiastic, 37f
  Greek, 29, 37f
Molière, 87
Monachus, 52
Monet, 167
monody, 35
Montesquieu, 114
Monteverdi, 20, 85f, 88, 93, 133, 160
Moore, 148
Morley, 77
Morton, 'Jelly Roll', 172
motet, 57
Milhaud, 129, 170
music drama, 160f
musica falsa, 56
  ficta, 56
  figurativa, 56
  mensurata, 56
  plana, 56

INDEX

vera, 56
Mussorgsky, 157f

neumes, 54
Newton, 100f
Nielsen, 169, 175f, 180
Nietzsche, 162
Nketia, J. H. K., 206
Nordraak, 153
notation, 54f

Obrecht, 64f
O'Carolan, 148
Ockegham, 63ff
Odington, 56
Offenbach, 142
Ogdon, J., 207
Orff, C., 176, 189
organum, 50ff

Pachelbel, 111
Paderewski, 114, 174
Paganini, 142
Palestrina, 14, 17f, 19, 57, 65, 67ff, 76, 85
Palladio, 67
Partos, O., 205
Pavlov, 8
Penderecki, 182
Pepusch, 99
Pepys, 78, 99
Percy, Bishop, 138
Pergolesi, 170
Peri, 14, 83f, 86, 116
Perotin, 52, 56
Peterkin, N., 194
Petrarch, 57
Philips, 84
pibroch, 23ff
Piccini, 115f
Pius IV, 71
Pipkov, L., 182
Pizzetti, 40, 194
Plato, 31
Plekhanov, 168, 181
polyphony, 10, 12, 13f, 16, 17ff, 76
Pothier, 40
Poulenc, 149, 170
Pound, E., 42, 44, 207
Praetorius, 93
Prokofiev, 179, 181
prolatio, 68
Ptolemy, 30
Purcell, 89ff, 102, 114
Pythagoras, 27f, 67, 101

Quinault, 88
Quilter, 194

raga, 13, 32f
Rakhmaninov, 172, 175
Ravel, 154, 167
Read, Sir H., 200
Reger, 169
Reicha, 135f, 188
Renoir, 167
Respighi, 40, 179
rhythm, 9ff, 12f, 15
Richard the Lion Heart, 43
Richter, J., 144
Richter, S., 181f
Rimsky-Korsakov, 157f, 175
Rinuccini, 83, 93
Riquier, 45
Roberton, 50
Robeson, Paul, 197
Robespierre, 139
Rodin, 48
Rosseter, 80
Rossini, 86, 149, 154f
rounds, 53
Roussel, 194
Rousseau, 114f, 141
Rozhdestvensky, 193
Rubbra, E., 194
Rubens, 112
Rubinstein, 141, 158f
Rufer, J., 182, 185
Ruskin, 68
Russell, 27

Sachs, 46
Saint-Saens, 140
Salieri, 134f
Sand, 151
Sandberg, 178
Sappho, 145
Sarngadeva, 32
Satie, 168, 177
Sax, 11
Scales, gapped, 33
 heptatonic, 26
 pentatonic, 24, 33, 34
Scarlatti, A., 94
Scarlatti, D., 94f, 96, 100
Scheidt, 111
Schoenberg, 17, 26, 64, 129, 167f, 169, 177, 178, 182f, 185ff
Scholes, 55
Schubert, 82, 103, 119ff, 127f, 131ff, 158
Schuller, G., 173
Schumann, C., 144f
Schumann, R., 103, 143, 144ff, 153, 173, 176
Schütz, 93, 133
Schweitzer, 93, 103f, 107
Scots snap, 147

Scott, C., 144, 167, 188
Scott, F. G., 178
Scriabin, 17, 168f, 187
Sechter, 133
Seeger, Pete, 193
Seiber, 173
Seter, M., 205
Shakespeare, 77, 89
Shankar, R., 33, 205
Sharp, 175
Shaw, 162
Shchedrin, 182
Shostakovich, 18, 102, 103, 158, 163, 179, 181, 182, 207
Sibelius, 174, 175, 179
Silvestre, 88
Simpson, R., 194
Skalkottas, 187
Smetana, 136, 152f
Smith, Bessie, 173
Smollett, 97
Smyth, 179
Somis, 31
Sonata da chiesa, 88f
sonata form, 123ff
Sophocles, 31
Sorabji, 203f
Spinoza, 112
Spohr, 135, 140
Spontini, 147
Stamic, 117
Stevens, B., 194
Stevenson, R., 207
Stockhausen, K., 188f, 191
Stokowski, 193
Stradivarius, 12
Stanford, 173
Stasov, 157
Steinway, 12
Strauss, J., 142
Strauss, R., 158, 169, 184, 189
Stravinsky, 169, 170, 177, 188, 189
suite, 121f
Sullivan, 142
Sviridov, G., 182
Sweelinck, 79f
symphonic poem, 161
symphony, 123
syncopation, 58
Szymanowski, 174f, 202f

Taglioni, 143
Tagore, 204f
Tailleferre, 170
Tatum, Art, 172
Tchaikovski, 158
temperament, equal, 101f
  mean-tone, 101
  Pythagorean, 101
Thérémin, 190
Tippett, 194
tonality, 100, 125f
Toscanini, 193
Tovey, 72
transcription, 84f
twelve-note composition, 185ff

Van Dieren, 194
variation form, 25
Vaughan Williams, 131, 179
Verdi, 86, 154ff
Victoria, 72f
Villa-Lobos, 176
Vivaldi, 94
Vladigerov, P., 182
Vogelweide, 46
von Bülow, 160
von Herbeck, 152
Voříšek, 136

Wagner, C., 160
Wagner, P., 36
Wagner, R., 15, 19, 46, 116, 143, 146, 154, 155, 159ff, 163, 182, 185
Waller, 'Fats', 172
Walter, 193
Walton, 194
Wang, 34
Warlock, 56, 194
Weber, B. C., 103
Weber, C. M. F. E. von, 141, 159
Webern, 186
Weill, 173, 195
Wellesz, E., 26
Wells, H. G., 27
Werckmeister, 100ff
Whitman, 8, 9, 178, 193
Widor, 158
Wieprecht, 11
Wilde, 149
Willaert, 65, 73
Wolf, 162f
Wordsworth, W., 194

Yasser, J., 198
Yeats, 91
Yonge, 75
Ysaÿe, 66

Zacconi, 70
Zarlino, 70, 101
Zhdanov, 180
Zola, 164